Emotions in Digital Interactions

Irene Rafanell • Maja Sawicka

Emotions in Digital Interactions

Ethnopsychologies of Angels' Mothers in Online
Bereavement Communities

Irene Rafanell
Division of Social Sciences
University of the West of Scotland
Paisley, UK

Maja Sawicka
Institute of Sociology
University of Warsaw
Warsaw, Poland

ISBN 978-3-030-21997-0   ISBN 978-3-030-21998-7   (eBook)
https://doi.org/10.1007/978-3-030-21998-7

This Palgrave Pivot imprint is published by the registered company Springer Nature Switzerland AG
The registered company address is: Gewerbestrasse 11, 6330 Cham, Switzerland

Preface

This book arose from the encounter between the authors, who saw in their collaboration a fruitful way to combine their respective theoretical and empirical work to enhance an understanding of the nature of social reality. This collaboration was underpinned, however, by a person-centered outlook about the life-world of women who have suffered an acute loss. The idea to go into the realities of their online communities was sparked during a conversation of one of the authors with a friend who suffered a perinatal loss. This accidental exchange of thoughts offered a glimpse of a universe of feelings regulated by a unique affective logic obscure for an outsider to this world. This book is an attempt to unravel this logic and translate this universe of suffering to those who might be oblivious to its very existence. In doing so, it attempts to reveal the varied nature and properties of the social world and its contextual grounding. Underpinning this work there are philosophical and ideological considerations aimed to contest, and provide an antidote to, forms of dogmatic essentialism which explicitly or tacitly silence and exclude individuals whose subjective experience, practice, and identity are made to be deviant or abnormal. The authors' collaboration emerged from a wish to not only advance academic and theoretical knowledge, but also to highlight the humanizing potential of a social constructionist position which aims to stress the right to being and existence of the marginalized.

This book would not have been written had not been for the bereaved women: courageous in their willingness to openly share the stories of their loss, and compassionate enough to support each other by exchanging their experiences. With this in mind, we would like to thank the anonymous participants of the online communities that we investigated, and—especially—those few who agreed to become our interviewees. In a sense, the analysis we present here is also *for* them: it is meant to give voice to their experiences and to reconstruct the internal logic which underlies their actions and feelings. We hope that it accurately depicts their plight and, by highlighting its sociological underpinning, somehow eases it as well.

Needless to say, this project would not have been successfully completed had it not been for the support of many people we met on our way, friends and family. We definitely owe much to Lynn Jamieson, who supported us both throughout the process of writing by unfailing confidence in our work, warmth, and friendship. We are also both indebted to our mentors Mirosława Marody and Martin Kusch, from whom we learned much about the aims, principles, and worth of sociological analysis. Part of this work was supported financially by the Institute of Sociology of the University of Warsaw (donation no. DSM-107700/16).

During the process of writing this book our personal family environment changed. One son left home to go to his own academic adventures and another was born to populate the nest of another home. We dedicate this book to our children, Samuel and Jerzyk, and our families and friends, whose support and insights were crucial in the process of writing the book.

Paisley, UK   Irene Rafanell
Warsaw, Poland   Maja Sawicka

CONTENTS

CHAPTER 1

Introduction

Abstract This introductory chapter outlines the theoretical framework developed, and the empirical investigation undertaken, in order to explore the emergence of a new ethnopsychology of motherhood in online bereavement communities. It adopts a constructionist approach which claims that new reality emerges from the coinage of new linguistic terms to refer to individuals' experiences. Key to this position is the claim that linguistic categories emerge as collective goods, i.e. social conventions. Such a claim, in itself, is not novel in the field of the sociology of emotions, which recognizes that emotions are both psycho-physiological and social in nature, and that social factors (including linguistic terms through which individuals identify and name their feelings) participate in the constitution of emotional experiences. However, the authors point out that such approaches perceive emotions as the *result* of social forces, neglecting their constitutive nature. Emotions not only emerge from social arrangements, but also act as *causal forces* that bring particular social phenomena into *being*. A central aim of the book is to identify the methods and mechanisms underpinning the emergence of a new emotional life-world. Such an approach builds upon symbolic interactionist and ethnomethodological tenets, further developing them by incorporating insights from the sociology of knowledge.

Keywords Language • Life-world • Sociology of emotions • Phenomenology • Interactionism • Ethnopsychology

© The Author(s) 2020   1
I. Rafanell, M. Sawicka, *Emotions in Digital Interactions*,
https://doi.org/10.1007/978-3-030-21998-7_1

The limits of my language are the limits of my world, noted Wittgenstein. This well-known statement can be interpreted as declaring that without categories which describe particular individual experiences, such experiences can pass unrecognized both by society and, crucially, by the individual herself. In this book, we aim to expose how, in order to make real a particular experience, collectives must have the adequate linguistic terms. When linguistic terms that are available to community members are inadequate to describe experiences, new terms must be created. We reveal how a particular subjective emotional experience becomes a reality by the coining of a new set of language categories, which allow it to exist. We do so by investigating online bereaved communities of women who have experienced perinatal loss. The core of this exploration rests on the tenet that the individual sense of an emotional experience being real emerges as a *collective convention*. Such collective conventions, we argue, are the product of dynamics of identifiable mechanisms operating in and through interaction, such as affective sanctioning, inter-group inclusion or exclusionary practices, and, in particular, the establishment of shared knowledge and linguistic categories. The aim of this book is to reveal the mechanisms by which communities of individuals, who do not find appropriate recognition of their subjective experience in their communities of origin, constitute new social phenomena to validate their personal emotional experience.

In the field of the sociology of emotions, it has been widely acknowledged that subjective emotional experiences are shaped by localized cultural factors (Denzin, 1990; Gordon, 1990; Hochschild, 2003; Lofland, 1985; Thoits, 1989; Wierzbicka, 1999; for an anthropologist account see also Wikan, 1990). Such an approach recognizes that emotions are not merely psycho-physiological phenomena but social as well. Social factors, such as linguistic categories through which individuals identify and name their feelings, participate in the constitution of the feelings themselves. The concept of ethnopsychology—that is, the emotional life-world that individuals share and experience together—captures the relation between cultural factors and the individual psychic structures that emerge from being embedded in a particular social context. In the understanding proposed by Thoits (1989), ethnopsychology encompasses the body of shared beliefs about emotions existing within a collective, including:

> rules regarding what one should and should not feel or express; ideologies about emotions such as romantic love; shared understandings of the typical onsets, sequences, and outcomes of emotional experiences and interactions;

socially defined exemption periods from expectations of emotional conformity; and beliefs about which emotions can and cannot be successfully con-
trolled. (Thoits, 1989: 322)

As such, an ethnopsychology circumscribes individual subjective emotional experiences with reference to the collectively held norms which
regulate feeling. In this sense, the concept of ethnopsychology is a useful
analytical tool to capture and understand the differentiation of emotional
subcultures, allowing light to be shed on the variable and changing nature
of emotional life-worlds. This is a sociological position which perceives
emotions as the *result* of the social context and the interactive dynamics
present in such a context (e.g. Gordon, 1990).

The concept of ethnopsychology allows for the identification and
description of phenomena such as norms, vocabularies, and beliefs, pertaining to emotions. In other words, *that* which emerges from social
dynamics in terms of what are to be the relevant emotions to be experienced by members of a particular ethnopsychology. However, important
as it is in terms of recognizing the social nature of emotions, such an
approach is not conducive to the understanding and explanation of *how*
these phenomena come to be, or how exactly they operate in generating,
patterning, and ordering the subjective emotional life-worlds.

In this book, we argue that emotions should not only be understood as
the result of social arrangements, but also as *causal forces* that bring particular social phenomena into being. We claim that a more in-depth
explanatory framework of the emergence of an emotional life-world must
uncover and identify those methods and mechanisms underpinning its
generation. Central to our position is the claim that *in* and *through* interaction, new forms of collective identity, and patterns of feelings and actions,
emerge. Such an approach explains an ethnopsychology as a collective phenomenon which goes beyond individual experience and derives from the
interactional micro-situational dynamics. Further, we claim that particular
methods, in particular affective sanctioning mechanisms, are key to the constitution of ethnopsychologies. In this sense, we argue that emotions
should be seen not only as outcomes of social dynamics, but also as pos-
sessing a key causal and thus constitutive role in forming social phenomena, including (paradoxically) emotions themselves. We present a detailed
analysis of how pride and shame operate as the methods which individuals
who have suffered perinatal loss use when they interact with others, and
which underpin the emergence of a local ethnopsychology of motherhood.

Our use of the concept of methods embraces, and further develops, the interactional approach. Symbolic interactionists, following Heidegger's phenomenological premise that the self should be understood as being in the world 'in the context of being with others' (Heidegger, 2011 [1927]: 152), have widely acknowledged the existential modality of the 'social', and defined individual subjectivity as emerging in and through interaction. Based on a long tradition emerging from the philosophical movement of phenomenology, particular schools of sociology have highlighted the profound significance of inter-subjective communication as the basis for the construction of social reality (Berger and Luckmann, 1991 [1966]). Ethnomethodology in particular, an interactionist approach developed by Garfinkel (1999), has provided a rich conceptual foundation to help understand how, through the dynamics of 'being with others', social life emerges. Ethnomethodology, as its name reveals, has placed emphasis on the 'methods' employed by individuals when interacting with each other, in order to make sense of each other's actions and accounts. Methods, in this context, have to be understood as the procedures, techniques, strategies, tactics, means, and routines which individuals use in order to successfully navigate such interactions. The 'ethno' prefix denotes both the fact that ordinary people engage in these kinds of methods in everyday interactions, and that they do so within *demarcated* groups. Thus, in ethnomethodological parlance, methods refers to the ways and means which individuals employ to produce stable and intelligible social order and smooth interactions. The suffix 'ology' implies the study or logic of these methods (Rawls, 2003: 123).

In applying such an understanding to the set of emotions existing within a demarcated group, we can likewise argue that those methods also order and produce the emotional constellation of said group, generating particular ethnopsychologies. This means that through such methods, feelings also become normalized—and thus commonsensical—within recognizable constellations of emotions to all the members of a community. In other words, these feelings become taken for granted and unquestionable for those members, and such normalized emotions become the background platform underpinning the set of emotional practices. More significant, however, is that such taken-for-granted categories of feelings, beliefs, and practices not only generate that which is to be taken as normal, but, consequently, define what is considered deviant. Becker, a symbolic interactionist author of similar methodological orientation to ethnomethodology, defines as deviant those who break the rules agreed by a group and, as such, they become outsiders (Becker, 1963). Therefore, deviance must be understood as relative in nature and linked to a particular set of rules and practices shared in a demarcated interactive collective. Following this framework, deviant (in the context of an ethnopsychology) denotes the individuals who do not follow or fit into the particular ethnopsychologies embraced by a community.

The phenomenon of emotional deviance was first described by Thoits (1990). She defines emotional deviance as 'experiences or displays of affect that differ in quality or degree from what is expected in given situations' (p. 181). Implications she sees for this concept are the ones she calls 'descriptive' (ibid.)—the empirical inquiry should, in her view, undertake the task of revealing who experiences deviant emotions (men or women?), when they are experienced (in what kind of situations?), and how often, and aim to describe the 'epidemiology' of emotional deviance. The theoretical implications Thoits points out are fundamentally psychological in nature and pertain to issues of individual motivation and the influence of emotion management on emotions: do emotions change under volitional influence? What does this tell us about 'the nature of emotion as a manipulatable biopsychosocial phenomenon' (p. 182)? These questions orient the inquiry towards *description* of populations, individuals, and emotions. However, such an approach falls short in explaining *how* the deviant and the non-deviant, what is considered normal and, by extension, divergent to the norm, are constituted in the first place. We argue that by investigating how the normal and the deviant emerge within a particular ethnopsychology, the methods underpinning the constitution of emotional life-worlds are revealed, as are, equally, how particular emotional experiences and feelings obtain the status of reality. The investigation provided in this book is, thus, a genuine constructionist exploration of social life.

In this context, the aforementioned Wittgensteinian statement acquires not only an epistemological nature, but also, crucially, an ontological one. It points our attention to the fact that linguistic categories not only provide individuals with means to describe and *know* reality, but, more significantly, denominate what *counts* as reality. When a community's life-world does not provide the individual with the language to make sense of, or express, her experience, then such a life-world does not allow certain subjective experiences to exist. This lack of linguistic terms effects an erasure of the subjective emotional experience from the social world and from reality itself. And, by the same token, if language exists to express individual experiences because they have become the property of a collective (i.e. are shared by all members), then a new life-world which allows for such experiences to exist is constructed. In both cases, the process demonstrates itself in the emergence of new language categories. As we argue later, a fundamental aspect of the emergence of new category terms should always be understood as the product of a collective of interactants, and never of a single isolated individual. In this book, we reveal how a particular subjective emotional experience connected to a perinatal loss—marginalized, disenfranchised, disqualified—within a particular deviant ethnopsychology of motherhood becomes normalized. This normalization will emerge by the creation and use of new linguistic terminology, which will underpin the reification of such feelings and of a redefinition of the content and meaning of motherhood.

We develop these premises in two parts. We first present the theoretical aspects of the debate and then move on to provide an empirical case study. In Part I, we present an analytical framework designed specifically to identify and understand the role of the methods through which communities generate new linguistic categories. We apply this analytical framework to investigate how communities who experience unrecognized emotional experiences in their social context of origin generate new linguistic terminology, to ground their emotional lived experience in the real world.

The analytical framework amalgamates insights from distinct theoretical approaches in sociology, such as ethnomethodology, symbolic interactionism, and the sociology of knowledge. Part I is structured as follows. We begin by providing a general background discussion on how social sciences have understood, and often left undertheorized, what is considered social (as opposed to individual). In order to uncover problematic adoptions of the understanding of what is social, we critically reconstruct two structuralist accounts: one which we call *extrinsic*, and the other which we call *intrinsic*. We argue that the latter provides a more theoretically developed and empirically substantiated understanding of the emergence of social phenomena. We then demonstrate how, in an intrinsic structuralist position, certain emotions are seen as central constitutive methods, meaning they are causal in nature rather than caused. Through this demonstration, the emotions highlighted as constitutive are shown to be those related to the dynamics of honoring and dishonoring the accounts and practices of members of a collective; that is, pride and shame. We focus on the latter, to show how social phenomena, in this case a new ethnopsychology, are also the product of such constitutive mechanisms. In

Part I, we also develop and identify different aspects of this process, including the role of language and the impact of affective sanctioning on the constitution of social reality. We continue by highlighting the open-ended and changing nature of social life. Finally, we end Part I by introducing the concept of a collective understood as a status group. The framework developed in this part provides analytical tools to identify and understand the interactional forces which underpin the emergence and constitution of a specific collective characterized by a deviant experience of motherhood.

Before we move on to Part II, we present the methodological underpinnings of the study and methods of data collection and analysis used. These are guided by the analytical framework developed in Part I. Informed by this framework, we are able to identify a set of key themes which emerge from the data and shed light on the dynamics of constituting a new ethnopsychology of motherhood. In the next step, we carry out a detailed, in-depth micro-analysis of digital interactions to reveal the interactional mechanisms which underpin these dynamics.

Part II presents the results of the empirical investigation into the emergence of a new ethnopsychology of motherhood among individuals deemed deviant by the prevalent ethnopsychology within their communities of origin. We pay specific attention to the new emerging terminology which, we argue, provides the ontological foundations for their subjective experiences in relation to their feelings of loss and grief. Different subsections present the empirical data according to thematic areas generated from analysis of the raw data. These revolve around identifying the exclusionary practices of the community of origin; the construction of a new community of motherhood; the emergence of the distinctive language necessary to recognize the experience of loss and grief of those individuals excluded by their communities of origin; and, finally, two sections which present the newly constructed realities of the unborn baby and Angel's motherhood as a newly defined and experienced type of motherhood.

We conclude by presenting both theoretical and practical implications of our analysis, in turn providing an enhanced understanding of the interactional processes, methods, and mechanisms through which social realities come into being. This is not only conducive to a comprehensive description of these realities and their internal dynamics, but also provides tools for practical procedures and interventions to be more effective when dealing with the emotional experiences of individuals affected by perinatal loss.

BIBLIOGRAPHY

Becker, H. S. (1963). *Outsiders: Studies in the Sociology of Deviance*. London, UK: Free Press of Glencoe.

Berger, P. L., & Luckmann, T. (1991 [1966]). *The Social Construction of Reality: A Treatise in the Sociology of Knowledge*. Harmondsworth, UK: Penguin.

Denzin, N. (1990). On Understanding Emotion: The Interpretative-Cultural Agenda. In T. Kemper (Ed.), *Research Agenda for Sociology of Emotions* (pp. 85–116). New York, NY: SUNY.

Garfinkel, H. (1999 [1967]). *Studies in Ethnomethodology*. Cambridge, UK: Polity Press.

Gordon, S. (1990). Social Structural Effects on Emotions. In T. Kemper (Ed.), *Research Agenda for Sociology of Emotions* (pp. 145–179). New York, NY: SUNY.

Heidegger, M. (2011 [1927]). *Being and Time* (J. Macquarrie & E. Robinson, Trans.). New York, NY: Harper & Row.

Hochschild, A. R. (2003). *The Managed Heart. Commercialization of Human Feeling*. Berkeley, CA: University of California Press.

Lofland, L. H. (1985). The Social Shaping of Emotion: The Case of Grief. *Symbolic Interaction, 8*(2), 171–190.

Rawls, A. (2003). Harold Garfinkel. In G. Ritzer (Ed.), *The Blackwell Companion to Major Contemporary Social Theorists* (pp. 89–124). Maden, TN: Blackwell Publishing.

Thoits, P. A. (1989). The Sociology of Emotions. *Annual Review of Sociology, 15*, 317–342.

Thoits, P. A. (1990). Emotional Deviance. In T. Kemper (Ed.), *Research Agenda for Sociology of Emotions* (pp. 180–203). New York, NY: SUNY.

Wierzbicka, A. (1999). *Emotions Across Languages and Cultures: Diversity and Universals*. Cambridge, UK: Cambridge University Press.

Wikan, U. (1990). *Managing Turbulent Hearts: A Balinese Formula for Living*. Chicago, IL: The University of Chicago Press.

PART I

Emotions, Social Interaction, and Structural Phenomena

CHAPTER 2

What Counts as Social Reality?

Abstract This chapter unpacks the concept of social reality. Referring to key claims of phenomenological, ethnomethodological, and symbolic interactionist accounts, the authors present the theoretical backbone of the analytical framework developed, which guides the empirical investigation. Central to their position is the assertion that the sense of reality and objective character of social phenomena are derivative of the constant, continuous work of individuals who cooperate to make things appear real. As Schutz and Garfinkel claimed, to achieve this the individuals must override inherent differences in how they individually experience the world. In this sense, a shared stock of knowledge (including linguistic terms) is a continuous collective accomplishment. Using the findings of sociologists of knowledge (especially Barnes and Bloor), the chapter highlights the process of reification of the social world. Such a perspective shifts the analytical focus to the methods through which individuals, in social interaction, produce and maintain their commonly accepted understanding of the world, and construct shared realities. Following Goffman and Scheff, the authors argue that emotions of shame and embarrassment are central to social dynamics and the constitution of social order. Affective sanctioning must be understood as a key constitutive method of social reality, and emotions as an essential structuring mechanism.

Keywords Ethnomethodology • Phenomenology • Social interactions • Affective sanctioning • Barnes • Garfinkel

I. Rafanell, M. Sawicka, *Emotions in Digital Interactions*,
https://doi.org/10.1007/978-3-030-21998-7_2

Following and expanding on phenomenological and symbolic interactionist tenets, ethnomethodologists have been crucial in shaping the methodological foundations of social sciences, in particular the study of the production of socially shared phenomena. They have provided key conceptual tools such as indexicality, accountability, practical action, practical rationality, and a collective stock of common-sense knowledge. Such analytical tools have been effective in challenging the existing structuralist account, which envisages the external social world as a 'metaphysics of substance'—in this case understood as a reified reality existing outside the lived experience and practice of individuals (Rafanell, 2021). Ethnomethodology followed Durkheim's premise that a 'social fact' appears as transcendental to the individual, and yet is the very product of the practical actions of a collective. In this way, the social fact is not to be understood as guiding individuals' actions, but rather emerging from them. Following the philosophical concerns of phenomenology, ethnomethodology helped the social scientific community to distinguish between *phenomena* (the perception of the world out there) and *noumena* (the objectified world 'out there'), and posed the radical premise that they are both intimately linked—that one does not exist without the other. More precisely, we should understand *noumena* as the result of dynamics present in the practices of everyday social experience, in particular those which make sense of the world within a community of interactive agents in ordinary life.

Schutz (1962) and Garfinkel (1999) advanced that humans action operates as a 'practical rationality'; that is, with the presumption that things actually are as they appear to be, and that we take the world of things at face value, rather than question its reality, foundation, or existence. Schutz and Garfinkel refer to this as the 'natural attitude', taken directly from Husserl's work on the understanding of how subjective experience constitutes the object it perceives, or what he called a phenomenology of experience (Heritage, 2008: 41). The natural attitude is understood as the making sense of objects, actions, and others during the normal, everyday practice of living, without questioning it. More significantly, Garfinkel in particular noted that this natural attitude does not unproblematically present itself in an individual's cognition, but rather, individuals work constantly to reconcile experiential discrepancies (ibid., p. 38). In other words, individuals, as members of the collective, operate within an existing stock of common-sense knowledge, which underpins such attitudes to the external world, founded in the permanent work done by individuals to limit such experiential discrepancies.

One significant aspect which Husserl highlighted in his investigation of the phenomenology of experience is what he named subjective structures. Put simply, these are inherent cognitive ways of experiencing the world. One such subjective structure is that individuals see the world as a perception of something existing in the world, independent of their conception of it. In this sense, Husserl points at the active role of sensory experiences in the constitution of the objects of experience (ibid., p. 39). Language itself operates similarly. Linguistic references always refer to something, to a substantive (understood in grammatical terms), and thus create the illusion that a material object exists prior to its naming. Therefore, the very same use of language generates, in our consciousness, the sense that objects pre-exist language, and that a reality exists outside and independently of individuals' accounts of it.

Following such phenomenological injunctions, Schutz and Garfinkel noted that a shared stock of knowledge is a contingent and continuous accomplishment of an empirically tangible and situated collective, and that individuals have to work at making things seem real and normal, by making sure they override individual discrepancies. The way that Schutz demonstrates this process is by noting that, confronted with the fact that individuals differ in their understanding and interpretations of things, they engage in 'the idealization of the interchangeability of standpoint', achieving a 'congruency of the system of relevances' (Schutz, 1962: 11–12). More simply, in everyday ordinary social interactions, individuals override the different perspectives each of them bring to a situation, by embracing a shared *idealistic* understanding of the social reality in which they operate. To understand how individuals achieve such idealizations, or construct a social reality based on such commonly accepted idealizations, Schutz, and subsequently Garfinkel, argue that social researchers had to study the ways (or methods) by which individuals, through social interaction, produce *and* maintain their commonly accepted understanding of the world. As described by Livingston:

> The central research problem is the examination of the unwitting, without extrinsic motivation, production of the ordinary social object. By finding what the practically accountable social object consists of as a produced object—as the achievement of its local production cohort—the ethnomethodologist simultaneously begins to find what it means to be a member of that cohort—that is, what a member of a production cohort actually is … It is this massive domain of practical methods, through which and wherein

people make of the things they are doing the things that they accountably are, that the ethnomethodologist seeks to investigate. (Livingston, 1987: 10, 11, 15)

Language and linguistic terminology command a central role in this process. If the phenomena perceived as real, obvious, given, or natural are the product of individuals working to make them so, then the appearance of reality is not a given emerging from the external world alone; rather, it emerges from the activity of a collective of individuals accounting for their activity with one another. Individuals produce accounts of reality in the hope of making it intelligible, reportable, analyzable, and/or describable to others. When others fail to understand such accounts, an individual's attempt to describe the world fails in its endeavor of making it real.

Further developments of the constructivist approach of ethnomethodology have been done under the banner of performative theories, notably those of Barnes (1983a, 1983b) and Butler (1990, 1993). These advances harnessed different constructionist approaches from diverse schools, such as the sociology of scientific knowledge and the philosophy of language (in particular Austin, 1970); and, in the case of Butler, the combination of the Austinian discussion on the performative force of certain linguistic acts with the Foucauldian theorization of power and knowledge as productive (constitutive of new social phenomena). Butler has argued that the constitutive powers of language, its performative force, are inherent in the fact that we use language *nouns*; that is, substantives which create the illusion that an external object exists prior to its naming (Butler, 1990: 18). Barnes offers a detailed conceptual apparatus, and descriptive account, of how the meaning attributed to linguistic categories is shaped and emerges from a community of mutually susceptible individuals, exchanging and modifying their personal interpretations to fit those of the other members. In doing so, they constitute the content, meaning, and role of the categories they use to describe and refer to the world; categories which also underpin the social norms, beliefs, and rules by which individuals of a collective abide. Barnes names his theoretical stance a performative theory of social institutions (PTSI, described later in more detail). One crucial aspect of the PTSI is that social reality is understood to be in a mode of continuous constitution and thus rendered open to negotiation, contestable and, consequently, transformable.

Barnes also provides a conceptual apparatus to further develop ethnomethodologists' emphasis on the production of social orders; that is, the patterning of individuals' practice. Barnes, as shown in what follows, extends from the patterning of individuals' practices to the constitution of social phenomena as the macro-world taken to be external by individuals and from individuals' actions. The PTSI provides an approach to explain how from individuals' practices, collectives produce a reification of the social. In particular, Barnes' theory provides detailed insights on how language is central to reality production. If we are to take seriously the phenomenological injunction that in order to properly and meaningfully understand a reality (social or natural), we must analyze in detail the operations by which objects appear as real to a community of individuals, then we must also focus on the role of language and descriptions of the world used by individuals as constitutive of it. Barnes' (1983a, 1983b) PTSI provides a thorough analysis of how labeling and referring are activities which, when conducted within a collective, possess a constitutive force.

Barnes' theoretical tools are particularly beneficial for the empirical investigation we undertake here, in that they help to elucidate how social reality is intrinsic to the micro-dynamics of collective action. Barnes' PTSI draws upon the work of another leading sociologist of knowledge, Bloor, to argue that all social reality constituted in the process of individuals engaging in interactive exchanges is open-ended. Bloor calls this meaning finitism (Bloor, 1991, 1997; Barnes et al., 1996). Meaning finitism is a position which recognizes that existing phenomena and objects in the external world do indeed have a causal impact on how individuals understand and refer to them, but only in an underdetermining fashion. The sociology of knowledge of Barnes and Bloor helps to counter accusations of pure idealism, which have occasionally been directed at ethnomethodologists (Maynard and Clayman, 1991), as though reality was nothing more than language and accounts made of it. It appears to be the case, however, that ethnomethodologists such as Garfinkel, in their attempts to prove the constitutive nature of accounts, ignore the causal impact of the external world upon those accounts. Bloor's meaning finitist account of reality helps to alleviate this perceived shortcoming, insofar as it develops an analytical framework that demonstrates the causal role of the external world, but in an *underdetermining* fashion. Such an analytical approach helps to unpack the mutual co-constitutive interplay between the external world and individuals' perceptions of it. Moreover, this analytical position demonstrates that linguistic categories, their meaning and content, and those external objects to which they refer, are always intrinsically open to modification and redefinition.

Much has been argued about the distinct nature of social and natural reality, and much sociology of knowledge scholarship has been dedicated to unpacking how both should be treated as socially constructed. Presently, we only wish to focus our attention on the methods and mechanisms used by individuals when constructing social realities. However, there seems to be some discord as to the nature of social reality, which can be described as those theorists of a positivist (realist) orientation—who conceive social reality as external and independent from individuals' perception—and the approaches of constructionists—who conceive social reality as emerging from individuals' perceptions, accounts, and practices (see Thomason, 1982).

Even for some of those theorists of a positivist orientation, the role of the internal dynamics within a collective appears central in how to understand social reality. For instance, the existence of intra-group dynamics of sanctioning among members of a group had already been identified by Durkheim (1982) in his early sociological theorization of what should be counted as a social 'fact'. Collective monitoring and controlling of individuals' deviant or differing attitudes, he noted, are central aspects in the existence of social reality as external to individuals' actions. Social facts, according to Durkheim, exist outside individuals' consciousness and exert constraint on their actions. This constraint may be recognized by the use of social sanctions, which reward compliance with a society's norms, rules, or beliefs, and punishing violations of or deviance from them. Deviations from social facts can result in different types of sanctions, formal (legal or institutional) and/or informal (commentary, judgments, evaluations, and reactions from others). Further developing a Durkheimian position, Goffman (1956) and Scheff (1988, 2000) argued that informal social sanctioning most commonly takes the form of affective sanctioning, in which the emotions of shame and embarrassment are central to social dynamics and the constitution of social order. The difference between Durkheim and Goffman and Scheff is that whereas for the former social reality constrains from the outside, for the latter the constraining (the dynamics of internal sanctioning) precede, and further constitute, social reality. In this book we take the constructionist position and, as such, we argue that affective sanctioning must be understood as a key constitutive method of social reality.

Emotions as a structuring mechanism highlighting the constitutive force of micro-situational dynamics have, however, been explicitly rejected by prominent social theorists (such as Bourdieu). Positions like Bourdieu's reveal a particular ontology of social reality (existing macro-structural arrangements) which envisages it as 'objective', external, and independent from individual action, thus mirroring the positivist orientation taken by Durkheim. This ontology tends to focus on how individual practice is determined by such external objective structures, rather than explaining how this external reality emerges in the first place. In what follows, we present an analysis of the constitutive role of affective sanctioning practiced among members of a collective, which reveals not only the theoretical weaknesses of approaches such as Bourdieu's versus those who acknowledge the constitutive role of social interaction, but also emotions as a key method guiding social interactions.

BIBLIOGRAPHY

Austin, J. L. (1970 [1955]). *How to Do Things with Words. The William James Lectures Delivered at Harvard University in 1955.* Oxford, UK: Clarendon Press.

Barnes, B. (1983a). Social Life as Bootstrapped Induction. *Sociology, 17*(4), 524–545.

Barnes, B. (1983b). On the Conventional Character of Knowledge and Cognition. In K. D. Knorr-Cetina & M. Mulkay (Eds.), *Science Observed. Perspectives on the Social Study of Science* (pp. 19–51). London, UK: Sage.

Barnes, B., Bloor, D., & Henry, J. (1996). *Scientific Knowledge. A Sociological Analysis.* London, UK: The University of Chicago Press.

Bloor, D. (1991 [1976]). *Knowledge and Social Imagery.* London, UK and Chicago, IL: The University of Chicago Press.

Bloor, D. (1997). *Wittgenstein, Rules and Institutions.* London, UK: Routledge.

Butler, J. (1990). *Gender Trouble: Feminism and the Subversion of Identity.* London, UK: Routledge.

Butler, J. (1993). *Bodies That Matter: On the Discursive Limits of Sex.* New York, NY: Routledge.

Durkheim, E. (1982 [1885]). What Is a Social Fact. In S. Lukes (Ed.), *The Rules of Sociological Method and Selected Texts on Sociology and Its Method* (pp. 50–59). London, UK: Macmillan.

Garfinkel, H. (1999 [1967]). *Studies in Ethnomethodology.* Cambridge, UK: Polity Press.

Goffman, E. (1956). Embarrassment and Social Organisation. *American Journal of Sociology, LXII*(3), 264–271.

Heritage, J. (2008 [1984]). *Garfinkel and Ethnomethodology.* Cambridge, UK: Polity Press.

Livingston, E. (1987). *Making Sense of Ethnomethodology.* London, UK: Routledge.

Maynard, D., & Clayman, S. E. (1991). The Diversity of Ethnomethodology. *Annual Review of Sociology, 17*, 385–418.

Rafanell, I. (2021). *Making up Bodies: Sexed and Gendered Bodies as Social Institutions*. London, UK: Palgrave Macmillan.

Scheff, T. J. (1988). Shame and Conformity: The Deference-Emotion System. *American Sociological Review, 53*(June), 395–406.

Scheff, T. J. (2000). Shame and the Social Bond: A Sociological Theory. *Sociological Theory, 18*(1), 84–99.

Schutz, A. (1962). *The Phenomenology of the Social World*. Evanston, IL: Northwestern University Press.

Thomason, B. C. (1982). *Making Sense of Reification. Alfred Schutz and Constructionist Theory*. Hong Kong, HK: The Macmillan Press.

CHAPTER 3

Emotions as Products of the Social: Extrinsic Accounts

Abstract This chapter discusses accounts of the social which the authors call *extrinsic structuralism*, and from which they wish to distinguish their own position. A central characteristic of extrinsic structuralist accounts is that they perceive social phenomena as independent from individual actions and the micro-dynamics of social interaction. Fully focusing on the causal force of macro-structural arrangements, they overtly or tacitly reject any constitutive power of interactive dynamics. In doing so, these approaches adopt a deistic understanding of the nature of the social world, in which the world is seen as created at some point and endowed by an inertia which guides individual activity. This stance is best illustrated by Bourdieu's concept of habitus, but also visible in some sociological explanations of emotions, for instance that of Gordon. The authors criticize Gordon's approach to emotions as unduly static, overlooking the constitutive role of the micro-dynamics of social life, and, therefore, failing to account for the link between social reality (an ethnopsychology, i.e. emotional life-world of a group) and individual experiences (emotions).

Keywords Social structure • Agency • Bourdieu • Gordon • Emotions • Ethnopsychology

Following from the discussion in the previous chapter, most sociological theorists appear to adopt, often unwittingly, such a realist orientation when it comes to social phenomena. When Durkheim famously proclaimed that social

© The Author(s) 2020   19
I. Rafanell, M. Sawicka, *Emotions in Digital Interactions*,
https://doi.org/10.1007/978-3-030-21998-7_3

reality has to be understood as a reality 'sui generis', he wanted to direct attention to the difference between social and natural kinds of reality. For him, social reality should be understood as both objective and external, and yet as, somehow, the product of individuals' actions. However, he provided no theorization on how social reality emerged, and adopted a rather radical positivist position which ultimately obscured his understanding of the objective nature of social phenomena (Rafanell, 2009). Social constructionist positions can be argued to be those positions which have attempted to theorize on the sui generis nature of social reality and locate at the center of their theorization the constitutive role of the micro-dynamics of individuals' actions. These theoretical positions have often been widely misunderstood, and criticized, as adopting a form of idealistic and anti-materialistic account and, above all, as neglecting the determining force of the existing macro-structural social order. This criticism usually takes on a strong positivistic flavor, in that it presupposes a 'real' world outside of, and informing, discourse and practice (Jackson, 1998). The critics have also accused social constructionist accounts as suffering from a form of voluntarism which dismisses the constraining force of structural phenomena over individual agency. Bourdieu takes this view when criticizing the performative theory developed by Butler in relation to the socially constructed nature of sex and gender identity:

> We have to acknowledge … the futility of the strident calls of 'postmodern' philosophers for the supersession of dualism. These dualisms, deeply rooted in things (structures) and in bodies, do not spring from a single effect of verbal naming, since the genders, far from being simple 'roles' that can be played at will are inscribed in bodies and in a universe from which they derive their strength. (Bourdieu, 2001: 103)

Bourdieu accuses constructionist theories such as Butler's of being a form of radical voluntarism which neglects the world of 'things' (structures) in favor of 'words' (discourse), something which amounts ultimately, according to him, to denying the existence of social structural phenomena. For critics such as Bourdieu, constructionists' theories are seen as purely idealistic approaches which neglect the constraining force of the external world, and pay no attention to structural givens. However, Bourdieu's critique suffers from a similar theoretical weakness as Durkheim's, in that they both presuppose a particular ontological understanding of social structures as existing prior to and independent of (and yet determining of) individuals' actions. These positions develop into a kind of sociological theorizing of social phenomena which we name *extrinsic structuralism*, which conceives structural phenomena as if already there, independent of individuals' actions (Rafanell, 2013). We argue that Bourdieu's criticism is founded on a misrepresentation of social constructionist accounts. In order to shed light on such misconceptions, we contrast these two positions in terms of how they understand the interplay between individual agency and structural phenomena. Such a contrast also reveals, crucially for the present discussion, their distinct conception and the role of emotions for social life, and in particular for individual practice.

While individual activity has commonly been accounted for in sociological theory as the result of the causal effects of the wider (social) environment, rarely has attention been given to how the macro-phenomena of such a structural world emerge. More often than not, it is taken as a given. There are two major theoretical positions that explain how order and consensus among individuals are achieved. As already noted, in Rafanell (2013) these two major theoretical approaches are described as extrinsic and intrinsic structuralist models. The first bases its premises on a deistic understanding of the nature of the structural world and how it informs individual action. Deistic creation approaches are understood as those which perceive the world as created at some point and endowed by an internal force, with an 'inertia', which guides subsequent activity (ibid., p. 3). This model translates into sociological theorizing in a similar way. In Bourdieu's own words:

> The opposition between, on the one hand, universes of social relations that do not contain within themselves the principle of their own reproduction and have to be kept up by nothing less than a process of continuous creation, and on the other hand, a social world carried along by its *vis insita* which frees agents from this endless work of creating or restoring social relations, is directly expressed in the history ... of social thought. (Bourdieu, 1995: 130, original emphasis)

Bourdieu's concept of habitus is a paradigmatic case in point of an extrinsic structuralist model: habitus is defined as a set of dispositional practices emerging from the early stages of socialization, which generate a set of dispositions permanently shaping individuals' actions and interactions, and, in doing so, automatically generate intra-group consensus and patterned social practices. An individual habitus is the product of what Bourdieu describes as 'objective conditions of existence', by which he means the structural world (Bourdieu, 1994: 170). These acquired dispositional practices, once constituted, proceed as in the deistic model, informing actions which 'can then subsist without agents having to recreate them continuously' (Bourdieu, 1995: 131). For Bourdieu, this model helps to explain not only the objective nature of the structural world, in particular its determining force, but also the internal dynamics between different groups of class habitus. Habitus dispositions generate individual practices which enable intra-group consensus; that is, consensus automatically generated among members who, by virtue of inhabiting similar structural objective worlds, develop similar patterns of action and perception. By the same token, such dispositional habitus practices generate intra-group conflict. This conflict is seen, by Bourdieu, as inevitable between groups (classes) because they operate in a totalizing hierarchy of differential values (capitals) which different class groups acquire in the social playing fields. Both intra-group consensus and intra-group conflict are thus the product of an external objective structural world which is conceived as prior to, and determining of, the actions of individuals. In other words, the intra-group consensus and conflict are *extrinsic* to the actions and interactions of individuals within, and between, class groups. Crucial to extrinsic models is the rejection of any constitutive power of individuals' interactive dynamics. Bourdieu is quite adamant on this:

> the notion of situation, which is central to the interactionist fallacy, enables the objective, durable structure of relationship between officially constituted and guaranteed positions which organized every real interaction to be reduced to a momentary, local, fluid order ... Interacting individuals bring all their properties in to the most circumstantial interactions, and their relative positions in the social structure govern their positions in the interactions. (Bourdieu, 1994: 578)

Orderliness, consensus, and agreement are, for extrinsic structuralist positions such as Bourdieu's, never the product of micro-dynamics, but rather that of the causal force of the macro-structural world. In this way, they clearly grant exclusive determining force to the external macro-world, adopting what can be seen as an overly determinist account of individuals' practices, agency, and behavior, and one which forecloses awareness and calculative action:

> The objective homogenizing of group or class habitus that results from homogeneity of conditions of existence is what enables practices to be objectively harmonized without any calculation or conscious reference to a norm and mutually adjusted in the absence of any direct interaction, or a fortiori, explicit co-ordination. The interaction itself owes its form to the objective structures that have produced the dispositions of the interacting agents, which continue to assign them their relative positions in the interaction and elsewhere. (Bourdieu, 1995: 58–9)

The interactions, which are accepted at their face value by people of an empir-icist disposition, conceal the structures that are realized in them. It is one of those cases in which the visible, that which is immediately given, conceals the invisible which determines it. One thus forgets that the truth of the interac-tion is never entirely to be found in interaction. (Bourdieu, 1990: 127)

What Bourdieu encapsulates with the concept of habitus are general dis-positions to act and feel, which are the result of existing objective macro-structural factors. This understanding is tacitly adopted in some significant works within the field of sociology of emotions: emotions are seen as shaped by macro-social factors (e.g. structural) and, if social interactions are taken into account, they are put into such an extrinsic 'macro' frame. Such an orientation is clearly visible in the following account by Gordon (1990):

Social structural effects on emotion flow through at least three interactional processes. In emotion differentiation, societies and subgroups distinguish in their language and social behavior among many types of emotions. Forms of anger can be culturally defined as annoyance, irritation, rage, fury, bitter-ness, jealousy, or vengeance, for example, each leading to different social interaction patterns. Through socialization, individuals learn to feel, attend to, express, and recognize the particular emotions identified in their society. Finally, the management of sentiments is the regulation of both expression and feeling according to norms of appropriateness. (p. 151)

For Gordon, such an approach to emotions is more 'social' than the one offered by symbolic interactionism, which, in his view, focuses merely on 'the social construction of emotions in face-to-face interactions and relationships' (p. 145). However, Gordon does not acknowledge that such a macro-social perspective largely overlooks how the external macro-world is generated in the first place and the constitutive role of micro-dynamics of social life, and, in doing so, fails to account for the link between social reality (an ethnopsy-chology) and individual (experiences-emotions). In fact, it offers a very static view of social life, in which individuals are molded into socially expected and relatively fixed 'emotional styles', through the power of socialization and social control forcing them into the types of emotion management which fit into the norms of their group. In this sense, Gordon unwittingly adopts a deistic and extrinsic model when conceptualizing emotions.

In contrast to the account presented by Gordon, we argue for a deeper explanatory and analytically precise framework which helps to elucidate the emergence of an emotional life-world, and identify those methods, processes, and mechanisms at play underpinning its generation. In doing so, we develop a theoretical model which conceives the structural world as the product of internal and situated micro-interaction dynamics. With this analytical approach we reject the 'once-and-for-all creation', deistic accounts of the social world, and instead adopt one that envisages social phenomena as in 'continuous creation'. Different social constructionist schools such as ethnomethodology, symbolic interactionism, and certain schools of sociology of knowledge adopt, to varying extents, this model. What we present in this book is an analytical framework which combines elements from these three approaches. At its core is the conception that the social world is created and *maintained* by the continuous activity of mutually susceptible individuals interacting with one another, and, in the process, generating alignment, consensus, and the ensuing collective social 'facts'. This position, as already noted, has often been misinterpreted as neglecting the determining role of existing structural/material factors. Contesting such a critique, we present evidence that this evaluation is misplaced and demonstrate that, on the contrary, there is no such neglect, but rather a different understanding of determinism and causality. We argue that the determining force (i.e. the norms, rules, and social orders) of the structural (or material 'objective') world exists, but must be seen as *underdetermining* individuals' actions, and that ultimately it is the force of the micro-dynamics of individuals' interactions which will fully determine action, interaction, and the social phenomena which circumscribe them.

Adopting such a model is key to understanding emotions differently to the extrinsic accounts, in that particular types of emotions are seen as constitutive of the social, rather than caused by it. In the same vein, all types of emotions and emotional life-worlds are to be conceptualized as emerging from the micro-dynamics of social interaction, rather than constituted by externally conceived macro-structural phenomena.

BIBLIOGRAPHY

Bourdieu, P. (1990). *In Other Words* (L. J. D. Wacquant, Trans.). Cambridge, UK: Polity Press.

Bourdieu, P. (1994 [1982]). *Distinction. A Social Critique of the Judgement of Taste*. London, UK: Routledge.

Bourdieu, P. (1995 [1980]). *The Logic of Practice*. Cambridge, UK: Polity Press.

Bourdieu, Pierre (2001 [1998]) *Masculine Domination*. Cambridge: Blackwell.

Gordon, S. (1990). Social Structural Effects on Emotions. In T. Kemper (Ed.), *Research Agenda for Sociology of Emotions* (pp. 145–179). New York, NY: SUNY.

Jackson, S, and Jones, J. (1998) *Contemporary Feminist Theories*. Edinburgh, UK: Edinburgh University Press.

Rafanell, I. (2009). Durkheim and the Performative Model: Reconfiguring Social Objectivity. In G. Cooper, A. King, & R. Rettie (Eds.), *Sociological Objects: The Reconfiguration of Social Theory* (pp. 59–76). Farnham, UK: Ashgate.

Rafanell, I. (2013). Micro-Situational Foundations of Social Structure: An Interactionist Exploration of Affective Sanctioning. *Journal for the Theory of Social Behaviour, 43*(2), 181–204.

CHAPTER 4

Emotions as Constitutive Methods: An Intrinsic Account of the Social

Abstract This chapter develops the authors' *intrinsic structuralism* position, which contends that social reality emerges in interactions between mutually susceptible individuals. It harnesses Barnes' performative theory of social institutions (PTSI), according to which the content and meaning of linguistic categories (and social institutions) emerge from acts of references to a given object made by a collective of interacting individuals. Secondly, the authors draw upon Bloor's meaning finitism, which states that linguistic categories, practices, and social phenomena at large are never fully determined by existing structural arrangements. Meanings which linguistic categories carry are thus open-ended in character and in permanent transformation, and so is social reality. Full determination emerges through the normative standards attained by the constraining force of inter-evaluative dynamics among the members of a collective. This leads to a focus on the nature of evaluative practices and to Scheff's theory of a deference-emotion system. Scheff states that shaming and priding practices underpin the constitution of patterned behavior. Consensus occurs when individuals, in order to avoid negative evaluations, align themselves to practices, norms, and knowledge held by other members of their communities. Thus, social life must be understood as ever-changing, in a *continuous* mode of constitution, and intrinsic to interaction.

Keywords Performativity • Meaning finitism • Deference-emotion system • Barnes • Bloor • Scheff

© The Author(s) 2020   27
I. Rafanell, M. Sawicka, *Emotions in Digital Interactions*,
https://doi.org/10.1007/978-3-030-21998-7_4

Collins, a prominent social interactionist, has persuasively argued that micro-situational activity should be seen as the 'ground zero of all social action' and proposes what could be interpreted as an illustrative intrinsic structuralist account. He points at two aspects of the priority of micro-situational phenomena. One is that we should understand that interaction dynamics is constitutive of macro-phenomena, but importantly too that this understanding of the role of interactive dynamics as constitutive provides a different conception of reality than that of the extrinsic accounts. His conception of reality is in fact more empirically founded than the latter, insofar as it conceives social reality as that which individuals in interaction *realize*, not as that which exists independently of individuals' interpretations and perception of it. It is in this conception of social phenomena that Collins' work resonates with the phenomenological and social constructionist positions:

> My argument is that microsituational data has conceptual priority. This is not to say that macrodata means nothing; but amassing statistics and survey data does not convey an accurate picture of social reality unless they are interpreted in the context of their microsituational grounding. Microsituational encounters are the ground zero of all social action and all sociological evidence. *Nothing has reality unless it is manifested in a situation somewhere.* Macrosocial structures can be real, provided that they are patterned aggregates that hold across microsituations, or networks of repeated connections from one microsituation to another (thereby comprising, for instance, a formal organization). But misleading macro "realities" can be built up by misconstruing what happens in microsituations. (Collins, 2000: 18, emphasis is ours)

Although there has been considerable amount of attention paid to the constitutive nature of individuals' interactive dynamics from interactionist quarters, few theorists have provided a more nuanced and analytically precise account of this process than Barnes. Barnes, a leading sociologist of knowledge scholar and founder of the strong program in the sociology of scientific knowledge (Barnes et al., 1996), which emphasizes the strong links between social forces and scientific knowledge production, has written extensively on sociological theory. In his more sociologically oriented work, Barnes has developed a range of analytical tools which are particularly useful to unpack and further understand the interactionist emphasis on the constitutive role of micro-situational interaction. His work is a paradigmatic case of an intrinsic structuralist model, highlighted by his emphasis on the role of language in micro-situational interaction as constitutive of social reality.

Barnes presents what he called a performative theory of social institutions, in a key piece of work which became the foundation of much of his subsequent exploration of sociological theory (Barnes, 1983a). In this piece, incorporating insights from Austin (1970) and other key philosophers of language and sociologists of knowledge, Barnes focuses on language and the use of categories to describe the world, and argues that individuals' acts of reference, within a community of interactants, constitute the reality which circumscribes their practices. A central point developed by Barnes' work is that patterned collective action involves the overriding and modification of routines at the individual level (Barnes, 2001). He emphasizes the collective as the constitutive base of all social phenomena, and criticizes much existing sociological theory for adopting a tacit methodological individualist bias, by failing to acknowledge the collective nature of all social life. Barnes provides a paradigmatic model of an intrinsic structuralism, which envisages social life as the continuous achievement of a collective of interacting individuals.

Barnes' use of the concept of the performative comes directly from the use made by Austin's developments of the philosophy of language, which sees some speech utterances as constitutive rather than descriptive; they change or create the reality to which they refer. They are performative, insofar as they constitute the reality they refer to 'in the course of the doing of an action' (Austin, 1970: 5), or, in other words, in the course of performing a linguistic utterance or act. This is not to be confused with Goffman's concept of performance of the self; that is, with an act of a single individual presenting herself to the world and managing her impressions to others. Performativity, for some social constructionist positions, is an operation of constituting the world in and through the referring to it, by individuals pertaining to a community of practitioners and knowers. Performance, in the Goffman sense, is the action of an individual to manage the presentation of their individual self, in the different situations in which they find themselves in the social world.[1] One of the key aspects which Barnes adds to this conception of linguistic utterances as performative is that they acquire their constitutive force *contextually*, only when they are shared and practiced by a community of situated, interacting individuals. Performative acts understood as the speech acts 'which bring into being that which they name' (Butler, 1994: 33) are an achievement of a collec-

---

[1] For an expanded elucidation of the differences between performativity and performance, see Rafanell (2009).

tive of interacting individuals negotiating, challenging, redefining, accepting, evaluating, and, in the process, aligning with each other and generating collectively recognized patterns of behavior.

4.1   LANGUAGE AND THE CONSTITUTION OF SOCIAL REALITY

Barnes' emphasis on the collective nature of performative speech acts is encapsulated in Bloor's description of the process: 'the reference of the predicate is a reality which is constituted by the *social* practice of making references to it' (Bloor, 1999: 109). In his work, Barnes presents an account of social phenomena as the product of the linguistic activity of individuals, *as long as* it is the product of a sufficient number of them making those referential acts, and is contextualized within a micro-situational context of individuals interacting. Barnes argues that any collective conventions, categories, or knowledge (all kinds of social institutions) are the product of interactive dynamics in which individuals constantly check their inductive inferences with one another, and in the process align themselves to each other in a manner through which collectively held knowledge will emerge. Social phenomena must be seen as the performative achievement of a collective of calculative, mutually susceptible individuals, making individually inductive inferences about the world which they will refer to. And, in doing so, they are collectively agreeing with one another on the adequacy and competency of their acts of reference, in relation to the world as they experience it. As he puts it, 'persons individually learning and confirming what they learn, [in and through acts of reference in which they engage] *collectively* create its reference' (Barnes, 1983a: 533).

A particularly significant aspect of Barnes' argument is that the object of reference (that 'external' object to which the particular predicates, nouns, and categories refer) emerges from the very practice of naming or referring to it. In this sense, social reality must be seen as self-referential in nature. To put it simply, the predicate 'mother' refers to something a collective of individuals take to be 'motherhood', and refer to as such. The object of the reference is thus emerging from all the acts of making reference to the object, and so is the specific content and meaning attributed to the categories used to refer to that object. The acts of reference constitute that which is taken to be the external object being referred to. With this analytical description of the self-referential nature of speech acts and its constitutive force, Barnes presents us with a particular ontological understanding of the nature of social reality, as that which exists within the linguistic usage of collectives of individuals, and not as an external entity which exists independently of individual practices. If a sufficiently large number of individuals partake in these acts of reference, what emerges is a reality 'sui generis', one which is the product of individuals' actions, and yet it presents itself as external to the single individuals.

This perception of externality is reinforced by the fact that deviant acts of reference are commonly put in check. This is how language reifies reality, a process which has been long acknowledged among key social construction-ist theorists. As Berger and Luckmann note, the very same use of language generates an actualization of the world in the subjective experience of indi-viduals, in that 'language is capable not only of constructing symbols ... but also of bringing back those symbols and presenting them as objectively real elements of everyday life' (Berger and Luckmann, 1966: 40). Once a collec-tive defines things as 'real then they are real in their consequences',[2] thus presenting a form of realism which differs from those of extrinsic accounts, which envisage the social world as separate and external from individuals' activity. In this way, social reality is reified as an objective given of discover-able structures and processes (Thomason, 1982: 2). In order to further clarify the constructivist conception of reality which we adopt here, it is important to stress that we are discussing *social* phenomena, rather than natural. Barnes' analytical unpacking of the constructive force of referential acts in terms of social and natural realities is helpful to further illuminate the nature of social reality.

Barnes' reasoning of how categories come to acquire collective life starts by detailing how both the categories which refer to the natural world (natural kinds of reality—NK) and those which refer to the social world (social kinds of reality—SK) have a referential component. In other words, in both cases, categories are used to refer to objects perceived as existing externally to the process of referencing. However, this process differs in an important aspect in the two kinds of reality. Whereas NK of reality have an external referent, existing outside of the act of reference (a tree, a rock, a tiger), SK of reality do not. In an SK of reality, the correctness of category designation relies not on particular traits of the external reality, but rather on the content and attributes ascribed to the social 'object' by the very

---

[2] This understanding of reality from Barnes and some key ethnomethodologists such as Schutz is encapsulated in the so-called Thomas Theorem (Thomas, 1928).

same community of referring individuals. Put simply, the content and meaning of a social category are that which the collective attributes to it. This is how a social category is to be seen, according to Barnes, as, due to the lack of an external referent, it just refers to itself. For example, a leader is what the community refers to and takes to be the leader, based on the particular attributes that said community grants to leadership. A married person is that which emerges from the particular social conventions and attributes of what is taken to be a marriage. Following from this, as we show in the empirical investigation presented later, what is to be referred as a mother should be seen in the same way: as that which a community of individuals take to be a mother based on the particular attributes which they confer to motherhood.

Category ascription often relies on the existence of an already used and accepted set of categories, which are frequently transmitted by accepted authorities (parents, teachers, scientists, religious leaders, etc.) or pre-existing social conventions which grant certain meanings to categories. However, Barnes notes that, as well as this existing set of pre-existing meanings, SK of categories are, more than in any other way, learned by virtue of being used and circulated through the exchanges which occur in the everyday interactions with others. The purely self-referential nature of SK of categories is demonstrated by this process of interaction, in which individuals learn what is to be referred to as something correctly, in the process of seeing how others refer to this social entity, rather than by external (to the community) existing attributes. In this sense, the same inductive process which guides category ascription of NK of reality operates in SK of categories. However, such an inductive process of inference takes a different form in SK of reality. Rather than observing the characteristics of an external object to confirm the adequacy of category ascription, in SK of reality individuals refer to how the other members of the collective make use of those categories to ensure correctness.[3] The collective is, therefore, essential in the process of referential activity, because it imposes the normative standards necessary to fix the content and meanings of particular categories. In doing so, the collective also underpins individuals' subjective experience. What is to be taken as motherhood will shape what experiences, and expected practices, the collective ascribes to *being* a mother. Individual acts of reference are thus *intrinsic* to the exis-

---

[3] This position directly resonates with Wittgenstein's argument that meaning emerges from the using of words in contextualized situations (Wittgenstein, 1953).

tence and maintenance of social reality; that is, social reality has to be understood as the product of the interactive dynamics of a *collective of mutually susceptible, interconnected* individuals.

The self-referential nature of such performative speech acts is also worth remarking on because, as we have already noted, it is a continuous and ongoing process—clearly revealed by the recurrent practices in which a collective engages in order to rein in deviant individuals. Referencing action occurs within ever-changing conditions, historically, politically, economically, and ideologically, and is also carried out by a collective of heterogeneous individuals, with differing personal experiences, backgrounds, and biographies. This inevitably carries the potential for, and often leads to, individually differing inductive inferences, and consequent deviation from the standard accepted meanings. The process of acts of reference is never totally fixed and meaning is never absolute; on the contrary, every act of reference is inherently open-ended and fluid. The meaning attributed to particular categories in and through the process of referring is also frequently disputed and challenged. Modified new understandings come to be negotiated, particularly when existing categories appear insufficient to describe personal experience.

Barnes' argument that social life is self-referential in nature very importantly highlights the fact that the process of reference, in its continuous nature, means that social phenomena are always open to modification. This point is of great significance, not only for understanding the nature of societal practices and phenomena, but also, crucially, for engaging in any effective empirical investigation into individuals' behavior. It does so by providing an understanding of the nature of social reality as provisional, and as the product of specific methods and mechanisms used by individuals to construct it; that is, to constrain, or at least minimize, the inevitable existing heterogeneity among individuals and create socially operational orders. A sound, informative, empirical investigation must aim to *identify* those methods which are used by individuals in their everyday life to achieve the emergence of this social reality. In what follows, we expand on these two key aspects in order to shed further light on the analytical advantages provided by an intrinsic structuralist model, one which does not take for granted the social but instead attempts to explain it. We start by further unpacking social life instability.

4.2   The Open-Ended Character of Social Life

As noted previously, a form of extrinsic structuralism such as Bourdieu's understands that once individuals' practices and actions are constituted as dispositional in a rather fixed manner by virtue of being conditioned by early life experiences, they are embodied in such a way that they become durable and bypass consciousness. This carries a particular conception of agency, which is a by-product of the structural world as individuals operate in the world without the need to make conscious, calculative decisions as they do so. This is because an individual habitus embodies (literally) the features prevailing in those external and objective conditions of existence, and therefore individuals' actions will always be in accord with such macro-structural requirements, creating no dissonance, and no need for any conscious calculative practice. In taking away the active and cognizant role of individuals in the interpretation, understanding, maintenance, and challenging of social reality, the Bordieuan position also conveys a conception of agency as, somehow, programmed to keep reproducing the existing social order and social hierarchies over and over.[4]

By the same token, consensus among individuals raised in similar social contexts ensues unproblematically, because similar conditions of existence result in habitus dispositions to act in similar ways. A habitus embodies similar predispositions to act, knowledge, beliefs, and views of the world. Individual practices (dispositions), once incorporated into an objectified habitus (in the sense of becoming reified in the corporeal), automatically generate intra-group consensus, resulting in an objectification of structural arrangements that 'can then subsist without the agents having to recreate them continuously … by deliberate action' (Bourdieu, 1995: 131).

---

[4] It must be noted that one of the main aims in Bourdieu's work is to propose a theory of power which explains the *reproductive* nature of social inequality and domination. Therefore, his efforts to propose a theory of practice with the concept of habitus as a set of dispositional actions respond to this aim. We believe that this explains his emphasis on revealing reproductive dynamics rather than in explaining change. In Bourdieu's view, individuals incorporate their own socioeconomic, contextual conditions of existence into a habitus, which is central in understanding the ever-existing class difference and class domination. Although the intimate connection between the practices implicated in the construction of society, and power dynamics, is in no doubt, this is an area of discussion which goes beyond the more ontological and epistemological focus of this book. It suffices to state, however, that Bourdieu's theory of power can also be seen as following an extrinsic structuralist model. See Rafanell and Gorringe (2010).

Although Bourdieu himself would deny that his model proposes any form of reification of the social which separates it from individual actions, this understanding of the social as fully determining individual practices involves a tacit understanding of the social as permanent and fixed (or as in a permanent mode of 'reproduction', as he puts it). Individuals' practices are conceived as re-producing existing structural phenomena, rather than constituting them. Individuals operate in the world unaware of its nature and take it for granted. This theorization clearly adopts a realist orientation which reifies macro-structural phenomena as independent of individuals' perceptions of them. As Thomason has put it:

> To treat social 'reality' as though it were already just 'there', independent of the sense *we make* of it, is to grant an improper thing-like givenness to the world and thereby necessarily distort and falsify its human constructedness. (Thomason, 1982: 1)

By denying the continuous role of individuals' actions in the maintenance of the social, implicitly Bourdieu envisages the social as extrinsic to individual action and, consequently, as *closed-ended*. That is, it is in a mode of inherent stability where change is only affected when exogenous factors are at play, such as when the society is invaded by external cultural and social forces, like colonialism (Burawoy, 2018: 61). In adopting such an understanding of the nature of social reality, an extrinsic structuralist model, which purposely rejects the role of the continuous activity of individuals at the micro level, fails to provide suitable analytical tools which can explain the ever-present change which societies undergo. More importantly, it leaves the 'social' unexplained, insofar as it presupposes the macro-structural world as an objective given, rather than explaining it.

Quite the reverse, an intrinsic structuralist model, such as that proposed by Barnes, highlights the open-ended and unstable nature of social life. In his explanation of the emergence of social institutions as the product of the referring acts of a collective of individuals, Barnes unpacks two key aspects of the nature of social phenomena: the key constitutive role of individuals' practices in interaction, *and* the methods and mechanisms used to effect stabilization and homogenization of the social world. Let us begin by indicating how social life necessarily has to be understood as open-ended.

In his explanation of the nature of SK of reality, Barnes asserts that individuals proceed inductively in order to make acts of reference. Individuals observe the world and, in the particular case of SK of reality, they observe others in order to ensure their referring acts are the correct ones. Two aspects must be highlighted in this process of the constitution of SK of reality, in and through language usage. First, existing categories and the content and meaning attributed to them only underdetermine our use of them. Therefore, in order to effect the necessary stabilization of the content of such categories, a mechanism of checking any disruptive deviations to the norm must be in place. Second, if a sufficiently large set of individuals do not find existing categories useful or suitable to their own personal experience, they often find ways to mediate the existing categories and modify them to more appropriately describe, and acknowledge, their own subjective inner world.

Barnes makes use of Bloor's theory of meaning finitism to further develop the point that existing categories (or norms and beliefs, for that matter) are never fully fixed in their meanings and content, and that individuals engage in particular practices which cause the stabilization necessary to be able to function in the world.[5] Meaning finitism (Barnes et al., 1996; Bloor, 1997) concerns itself with how linguistic meaning arises, the status of true or false statements, and how individuals learn to master linguistic classifications. Thus, it is a very useful analytical framework to harness when analyzing the use and emergence of new linguistic categories and the practices associated with them, as is the case in the empirical investigation undertaken in this book. Meaning finitism contends that individuals learn the correct usage of language in and through interaction with others, and that individuals of a collective actively engage in checking the deviant. As Bloor puts it:

> Collectively held normative standards come from the consensus generated by a number of interacting rule followers, and is maintained by the collective monitoring, controlling and sanctioning their individual tendencies. (Bloor, 1997: 17)

Why is interaction seen as so key by Barnes and Bloor when it comes to understanding how the meaning of a category is established? Meaning finitism is a position which argues that no previous or existing rule, norm, or content of a category can be identically applied on future occasions. This is because, however slightly, there are always differing conditions in

---

[5] Bloor, along with Barnes and other sociologists of knowledge, is a leading founder of the strong program in the sociology of scientific knowledge.

the contexts in which individuals operate. Individuals, indeed, learn and habituate themselves to particular meanings and use of categories within an existing context and background of knowledge and assumptions, but this habituation only underdetermines future practice. Changing conditions mean that future use of categories is always open to potential new meanings or interpretations of the situation at hand, therefore individuals constantly engage in calculative assessments, which they corroborate through the responses of others, if they are engaging in the correct use of language. In this process, individuals not only ensure the adequacy of their existing knowledge but also, significantly, keep relearning and readapting their responses to newly encountered situations. This is a continuous creation view 'that sees meaning as developing over time as terms are applied' (Kusch, 2002: 201). Since meanings are continuously made and remade, only the collective can generate the status of 'correctness' of an individual category ascription at a point in time.

Meaning (that is, the content ascribed to a category) must be understood as underdetermined. Meaning finitism states that meaning has intrinsically no fixed content from which individuals can draw unequivocally in order to guide their actions. As in meaning, individuals' practices and social encounters are never entirely fixed in advance, but rather are always revisable. What was found correct and useful in the past may not be so in future circumstances, in which new emerging conditions or knowledge, has generated changes, varying also individual and collective interests (Barnes et al., 1996: 57). It is therefore clear that individuals not only infer or learn from an existing pool of knowledge, frames of reference, normative standards, or common practices, but they *confirm* what they learn by checking with others that there is no discrepancy. In doing so, new modified meanings and practices emerge as contingent to fluctuating social circumstances, and individuals engage in a continuous readjustment and realignment with one another in the process of social interaction.

So, social life must be understood as ever-changing; in a *continuous* mode of constitution. This is not to deny the causal and determining impact of pre-existing social phenomena, rather, it is to say that pre-existing social factors only underdetermine and that, unlike Bourdieu's extrinsic structuralist model, which conceives social life as constituted at one point once and for all, an intrinsic structuralist model, like the one proposed by Barnes, conceives social life as in *continuous creation*.

The intrinsic structuralist model of understanding social life is open-ended in nature, and offers a more dialectical account of the relationships between the co-constitutive feedback loop between existing macro-phenomena and individuals' micro-activity. This is not to deny that, often, certain social practices, norms, beliefs, and so forth do not show a high degree of stability or are not being reproduced. It just means understanding the nature of the reproduction of existing social orders differently than that of extrinsic structuralist accounts. Certain social institutions (or linguistic categories or practices, norms, or beliefs) appear to remain rather unaltered over time. For instance, the binary division of sex identity into male and female could be considered one very stable social reality across time. This stability, however, should not be understood as provided by an external factor, let us say the biological given features of different reproductive organs, but rather as the product of a large number of individuals accepting this interpretation of sex 'identity', as based in this particular biological aspect, and constantly referring to it as such.

Social institutions of this nature, which evidence a high degree of stability, emerge when they become heavily protected by the members of a society. Such social institutions are normally those which become part of the taken-for-granted realm and they are rarely contested as such. However, they exist in this form because individuals of a community actively engage in negatively sanctioning any individuals who deviate from what the community deems 'natural' and 'commonsensical' and therefore independent of social conventions. When certain social institutions take this form of self-evident and immutable truth, any radical or even minimal deviation from it generates serious opposition, criticism, and attack, deterring deviation and further ensuring its reinforcement and reproduction. Although such large social institutions may appear to the single individual as existing outside the collective dynamics, they are in fact the product of the constant reinforcement of all members of the community.

A key aspect that the intrinsic structuralist position highlights is the constitutive role of the evaluative judgments which individuals constantly engage in towards one another. The inter-dependent nature of individuals has been stressed in many social constructionist accounts, since philosophical phenomenology highlighted inter-subjectivity as key to the development of human consciousness. What is significant for the present discussion is the particular nature of this inter-dependence, which Barnes, no doubt building upon existing interactionist accounts, describes as mutual susceptibility to the reactions of others:

Human beings can ride in formation, not because they are independent individuals who possess the same habits, but because they are interdependent social agents, linked by a mutual susceptibility, who constantly modify their habituated individual responses as they interact with others, in order to sustain a shared practice. (Barnes, 2001: 37)

In this framework, it is important to emphasize that the mutual susceptibility of individuals to signs of approval and disapproval operates within particular contextualized and situated settings of group boundaries. Individuals are susceptible to approval and disapproval from those with whom they have face-to-face, direct interactions, but particularly from those individuals to whom they have granted particular social statuses. Traditionally we understand such individuals as those who have been granted particular social status, such as parents, teachers, bosses, popular and professional peers, and so on. However, symbolic interactionists have long recognized that individuals are most susceptible to evaluation from others with whom they share, or strive to share, a group identity. Group belonging is central in manifold ways in social life, but one aspect to highlight for the purpose of the present study is the tendency of individuals to avoid negative evaluations, particularly from members of groups they strive to belong to. Evaluative judgments can take many forms, but inherent in all appraisals are the positive and negative actions and declarations towards others. In doing so, a group boundary emerges, as well as the normative standards guiding action and generating consensus among the members of the group. As Bloor notes, 'consensus makes norms "objective", that is, [they are perceived as] a source of external and impersonal constraint on the individual' (Bloor, 1997: 17). In this sense then, this type of sanctioning must be considered a fundamental method that individuals use in their interactions, which results in the constitution of social reality. We will now discuss what interactionist scholars have considered one of the key methods to ensure consensus and agreement, that is, *affective* sanctioning.

4.3   AFFECTIVE SANCTIONING AND SOCIAL ORDER

Let us recapitulate the main aspects of the discussion so far in regard to the emergence and nature of social reality from an intrinsic structuralist position. Such a theoretical model contents that social life must be understood as emerging from the micro-interactions among individuals in situated contexts, and it can be summarized in the following key points:

- Acts of reference are performative in nature and have a constitutive effect, but only when they are the product of a collective of individuals.
- Linguistic categories, practices, and social phenomena at large are never fully determined by previous socialization, usage, or existing standards. They are open-ended in character and in permanent transformation, because social reality never exists in identical forms.
- Individuals are heterogeneous by nature, but are mutually susceptible to evaluations from others. Consensus occurs when individuals, in order to avoid negative evaluations, align themselves to the practices, norms, and knowledge held by the other members of the community in which they interact. This generates a homogenization of individuals' accounts, which in turn results in individuals perceiving the social world as independent from their accounts of it.

It is to the latter that we now turn our attention; that is, to the nature of those evaluations in which individuals engage, and, in particular, the forms which such evaluations take. Durkheim's early theorization of the nature of social reality already hinted that the presence of forms of sanctions pointed to the very existence of social reality. A 'social fact', Durkheim stated, was identifiable 'through the power of external coercion which exerts ... upon individuals ... the presence of this power is in turn recognizable because of *the existence of some predetermined sanction* or through the resistance that the fact opposes *to any individual action that may threaten it*' (Durkheim, 1982: 59). However, what the social constructionists, in the hands of ethnomethodologists, symbolic interactionists, and sociologists of knowledge such as Barnes, have contributed to this debate is an important re-examination of the emergence of social reality. All these approaches share the general conception that social reality cannot be understood as an existing objective given, guiding individual practice from the outside, but rather must be seen as the product of micro-situational action, and cannot exist independently of individuals' practices. In doing so, they have explained away the more positivistic leanings of the Durkheimian approach and many subsequent structuralist approaches—such as that of Bourdieu noted earlier—whose models appear to adopt a particular version of reification akin to a platonic realism, thus tacitly rendering social reality ahistorical and totalized. We label the latter extrinsic structuralism, insofar as it conceives the structural world as somehow independent from individual practice and operating from the outside, which can be discovered in an analogous way to physical objects in the natural world.

The intrinsic model we present here does not represent a form of idealism which does not account for or acknowledge the existence of structural phenomena. On the contrary, what an intrinsic model proposes is a different understanding of how social reality becomes reified; that is, as perceived as objectified from the subjective experiences of individuals and yet being the product of them. Barnes' account, in particular, provides a detailed description of the process of emergence of social reality which locates individual action at its core. The meaning finitist's claim that socializing forces, and existing norms and knowledge, only underdetermine behavior and cannot fully account for the existence of consensus among a collective of individuals has significant implications for the present discussion, insofar as it sheds light on the fact that social reality is the product of the consensus and agreement generated by the individuals of a collective.

This understanding, that consensus and agreement are *achieved* and exist in society, has been widely acknowledged from many different sociological quarters, notably by Parsons and functionalist perspectives—within which we also locate Bourdieu—which envisage primary socialization, in particular the family, as shaping individuals' future practice and thus explaining social stability. Contrary to this view, the intrinsic model we present here contends that consensus and agreement cannot be understood as the sole product of an early internalization of social norms and beliefs, but rather as a continuous achievement of mutually susceptible individuals engaging in constant interpretation and verification of their individual practice. Individuals operate within an existing background of existing knowledge, norms, beliefs, and tendencies to act in certain ways, which inform individual inferences, but these inferences are by nature, as Bloor has argued, provisional and open-ended. It is not until the collective corroborates them that they become fixed and stable, thus acquiring the nature of 'objective' reality. Bloor notes that in order for this to be the case, 'we need methods for sanctioning and modifying our individual dispositions to keep them in line' with those of others, and that individuals do so by the constant mediation and evaluation of others, 'by verbal commentary, criticism and evaluation; e.g. by saying you can or you must' (Bloor, 2001: 101). By invoking the existence of methods as key to the constitution of consensus and patterned social life, Bloor shares the same methodological concerns as ethnomethodologists such as Schutz and Garfinkel, who insisted in the study of the ways in which individuals in interaction produce *and* maintain their collective understanding of the world and social reality.

Social sanctions to stop deviation and produce alignment between individuals can be both formal (e.g. legal or institutional systems) and informal. Barnes and Bloor point at the ubiquitous existence of informal sanctioning, without which shared knowledge and the social world could not exist or emerge. Informal social sanctioning can take many forms, but a key informal sanctioning method for the constitution and maintenance of social phenomena and patterned individual practice, highlighted by Goffman and further developed by Scheff, is that of affective sanctioning. The specific affective dimensions these two authors point to are those which take the form of pride and shame.

While Goffman brought into sharp relief the key role of embarrassment in social organization (Goffman, 1956), his discussion remained largely focused on the individual's subjective experience in relation to others in social interaction, rather than on how embarrassment is constitutive of the social. Goffman sees embarrassment as something individuals attempt to avoid in order to manage their 'impression' towards others, as a way to generate an acceptable and operational sense of self within the community in which they operate. In doing so, individuals adapt to what they think is expected of them and, in turn, protect and constitute not only their own sense of self, but also the orderliness of the social interaction itself. Embarrassment then, according to Goffman, has a social function:

> In every social system, however, there are times and places where audience segregation regularly breaks down and where individuals confront one another with selves incompatible with the ones they extend to each other on other occasions. At such times, embarrassment, clearly shows itself to be located not in the individual but in the social system ... To this extent, embarrassment is not an irrational impulse breaking through socially prescribed behavior but part of this orderly behavior itself. (Goffman, 1956: 269–271)

Scheff's continuation of the Goffmian theorizing of embarrassment takes further the social dimension of embarrassment. Developing an extended theoretical discussion, Scheff focuses on the key constitutive role of affective sanctioning, in the form of priding and shaming, for the patterning of individuals' behavior and consensus generation. With this, he provides a deeper analysis of how the emotions of pride and shame act as constitutive methods, which, going beyond the intra-subjective realm of the single individual, act as mediators of the inter-subjective dynamics among individuals, underpinning mutual coordination and ultimately social life. In doing so, Scheff shares a conception of social reality with the other constructionist authors already mentioned, in that his analytical framework encompasses a commitment to both an objectivist view of the social world as the more positivist structuralists would have it, and to the methods of a subjectivist emphasis on everyday actors of the constructionists' positions.

Scheff presents and develops his position on a theoretical framework which highlights a process pervasive in all social interactions, which he names the 'deference-emotion system' (Scheff, 1988, 2000). His core argument is that that shaming and priding are at the core of the constitution of patterned behavior, by the fact that these are the emotions which underpin all human interaction. He argues that conformity to existing norms and beliefs is rewarded with appreciation and positive reactions (such as prizes, medals, or any kind of positive evaluation). These make individuals feel good about themselves and, as a consequence, more inclined to follow the normative standards of the collective in which they interact. By the same token, individuals are negatively sanctioned when they deviate or show non-conformity to commonly accepted norms and behavior, by being punished with negative evaluative judgments (often very informal, such as ridicule or lack of deference) which generate feelings of shame and embarrassment. These emotions are experienced as psychologically very difficult and painful, and consequently individuals tend to avoid them by falling in line with what is expected of them in their interactive contexts.

Scheff's development of the deference-emotion system is extensive and manifold, providing analytical tools that shed light on the development of individuals' sense of subjective self, as well as more sociological aspects of the emergence of social life. For the purpose of the present discussion, we focus on the latter. Scheff's core argument is that despite having low visibility in social encounters, shame should be considered as a 'master emotion', in that it has more social impact than other emotions. As he puts it, shame has a key social function, insofar as it regulates social bonds, since shame arises when these are threatened. In this sense, shame is central to social bonding and the construction of individuals' subjective sense of identity, in conformity to what is accepted by society, and individuals engage in constant self-monitoring, arising from checking others' perceptions of oneself and 'monitoring of one's actions by viewing one's self from the standpoint of others' (Scheff, 1988: 400).

With this, Scheff emphasizes the highly inter-dependent nature of individuals and their mutual susceptibility to one another. This results in shaping individuals' subjective sense of self and the practices which ensue in accordance with commonly held beliefs and practices. Scheff's analysis sheds light on how emotions such as shame and pride effectively function to guarantee the alignment of thoughts, feelings, and actions among individuals, thus constituting patterned behavior and social phenomena. A significant aspect that Scheff highlights is the compelling constitutive force of the affective emotion system, and, in particular, of shame, stemming from its taboo nature. Unlike other emotions, Scheff notes, shame, and the feelings of embarrassment that ensue, is a highly culturally hidden emotion. Even in social settings such as psychological therapeutic sessions, where emotions are discussed, shame tends not to be explicitly named. This is because shame is experienced in situations where individuals' sense of self-esteem, self-worth, and character is profoundly threatened and, consequently, their social status and worth diminished. This, Scheff concludes, generates a tendency to conform to norms in a manner of which individuals are hardly aware, and generates a form of 'social control [which] involves a biosocial system that functions silently, continuously and virtually invisibly, occurring *within* and *between* members of a society … in a situation' (Scheff, 1988: 405). In this way, he presents a clear account of social life as an intrinsic structuralist model which emphasizes the situational component of individual interactions, and its continuous creation mode of understanding social life.

Scheff's theoretical account of the constitutive power of priding and shaming also highlights the social bases of individual subjective life and self-perception. In and through this continuous self-monitoring, individuals generate a subjective sense of self, thus cultivating the necessary elements to make sense of their own experience. The existence of a background set of rules, norms, linguistic categories, and labels as those accepted and followed by a community of individuals abiding and agreeing to them engenders the possibility of the 'recognition' of one's own experience as commonly recognized as authentic and genuine, and therefore as 'real'. As noted by Barnes and Bloor, there is no subjective reality unless it is inscribed within a set of commonly held beliefs and practices. It is not until we recognize our subjective experiences as something shared by other individuals of a situated community of practice that we can name, and subsequently experience, our own subjective world, emotions, or even physical experiences.[6]

This leads us to consider those situations in which the experiences of a set of individuals are negated by the communities to which they belong, by virtue of a lack of terminological resources and practice-based actions which can provide the necessary recognition, and they are therefore denied their 'existence' in the world. Let us recall that Barnes' performative theory stresses that SK of reality are constituted in and through language use, and the acts of reference of a community of users. Bloor's meaning finitism theory stresses that this process always renders social life, as the content and meaning attributed to linguistic categories, open-ended: open to be redefined in ways which suit newly encountered situations. If a sufficiently large set of individuals who do not find adequate recognition of their experience in their communities of origin come to interact among themselves, they often find new ways to redefine the existing categories in a way that suits, giving credibility and existential weight to their subjective experience. The individually experienced phenomena, in the same fashion which operates in all social life, will acquire significance once they are confirmed with others experiencing similar situations. This confirmation will emerge though the process described earlier, through sharing, learning, negotiating, and confirming with others their individually experienced phenomena, generating new or modified linguistic terminology, categories, and practice. This will become the collectively shared good of this new community, and in turn individuals will have to abide by a new set of normative standards, if they wish to belong to the community. Scheff's, as well as Barnes and Bloor's, analytical tools, allow us to frame the empirical investigation presented in Part II on online communities of support for individuals who have suffered prenatal loss. In particular, it allows to reveal and investigate the process of emergence of new redefinitions of existing categories of motherhood. Which will allow for the subjective experience of loss of their members, that their communities of origin have difficulties in acknowledging or even disapprove of, to acquire significance and, ultimately, 'existence'.

[6]Becker convincingly argued that even the physical effects of marijuana are learned as experienced in particular ways in a situation of interaction with other marijuana users, in which individuals tend to follow the adopted script of the community rather than admitting what may be seen by others as ineptitude if they acknowledge a different experience (find the use of the drug unpleasant rather than pleasurable, for instance). Those scripts allow individuals not only to label their personal experience in particular ways (such as being 'high'), but shape their own physical experience to conform to other marijuana users with whom they interact. In doing so they are being rewarded by giving them the sense of 'belonging' to the group (Becker, 1963).

BIBLIOGRAPHY

Austin, J. L. (1970 [1955]). *How to Do Things with Words. The William James Lectures Delivered at Harvard University in 1955.* Oxford, UK: Clarendon Press.

Barnes, B. (1983a). Social Life as Bootstrapped Induction. *Sociology, 17*(4), 524–545.

Barnes, B. (2001). Practices as Collective Action. In K. D. Knorr-Cetina, T. Schatzki, & E. von Savigny (Eds.), *The Practice Turn in Contemporary Theory* (pp. 17–28). London, UK: Routledge.

Barnes, B., Bloor, D., & Henry, J. (1996). *Scientific Knowledge. A Sociological Analysis.* London, UK: The University of Chicago Press.

Becker, H. S. (1963). *Outsiders: Studies in the Sociology of Deviance.* London, UK: Free Press of Glencoe.

Berger, P. L., & Luckmann, T. (1966). *The Social Construction of Reality: A Treatise in the Sociology of Knowledge.* Harmondsworth, UK: Penguin.

Bloor, D. (1997). *Wittgenstein, Rules and Institutions.* London, UK: Routledge.

Bloor, D. (1999). Anti-Latour. *Studies in History and Philosophy of Science, 30*(1), 81–112.

Bloor, D. (2001). Wittgenstein and the Priority of Practice. In T. R. Schatzki, K. Knorr-Cetina, & E. von Savigny (Eds.), *The Practice Turn in Contemporary Theory.* London, UK: Routledge.

Bourdieu, P. (1995 [1980]). *The Logic of Practice.* Cambridge, UK: Polity Press.

Burawoy, M. (2018). Making Sense of Bourdieu. *Catalyst, 2*(1), 51–87.

Butler, J. (1994). Gender as Performance. An Interview with Judith Butler. *Radical Philosophy, 67*, 32–39.

Collins, R. (2000). Situational Stratification: A Micro-Macro theory of Inequality. *Social Theory, 18*(1), 17–43.

Durkheim, E. (1982 [1885]). What Is a Social Fact. In S. Lukes (Ed.), *The Rules of Sociological Method and Selected Texts on Sociology and Its Method* (pp. 50–59). London, UK: Macmillan.

Goffman, E. (1956). Embarrassment and Social Organisation. *American Journal of Sociology, LXII*(3), 264–271.

Kusch, M. (2002). *Knowledge by Agreement.* Oxford, UK: Oxford University Press.

Rafanell, I. (2009). Durkheim and the Performative Model: Reconfiguring Social Objectivity. In G. Cooper, A. King, & R. Rettie (Eds.), *Sociological Objects: The Reconfiguration of Social Theory* (pp. 59–76). Farnham, UK: Ashgate.

Rafanell, I., & Gorringe, H. (2010). Consenting to Domination? Theorising Power, Agency and Embodiment with Reference to Caste. *The Sociological Review, 58*(4), 604–622.

Scheff, T. J. (1988). Shame and Conformity: The Deference-Emotion System. *American Sociological Review, 53*(June), 395–406.

Scheff, T. J. (2000). Shame and the Social Bond: A Sociological Theory. *Sociological Theory, 18*(1), 84–99.

Thomas, W. I. (1928). *The Child in America: Behavior Problems and Programs.* New York, NY: Knopf.

Thomason, B. C. (1982). *Making Sense of Reification. Alfred Schutz and Constructionist Theory.* Hong Kong, HK: The Macmillan Press.

Wittgenstein, L. (1953). *Philosophical Investigations.* Oxford, UK: Blackwell Publishing.

CHAPTER 5

Emergence of Collectives as Status Groups

Abstract In this chapter the concept of status groups is introduced. The claim that collectives operate as status groups is central to the intrinsic structuralist model. Status groups are understood here as communities of a common language and concepts, which develop a distinctive 'culture' based on the adoption of shared collective properties. Their members share and recognize particular markers of honor and prestige which become status group *markers*. Status group markers delineate and constitute group boundaries: possession or not of the group's status markers distinguishes the insiders from the outsiders and thus members from non-members. The basic assumption is that status markers operate as collective goods and they are always situated and contextual. This means that exclusion from a group results in the loss of certain forms of social identity, and of access to the given reality adopted by such groups. According to the intrinsic structuralist position, status markers are contingent and fluid—they must be continuously maintained by the interacting collective. Identifying the process by which such status markers emerge is key to understanding individual practice, group dynamics, and social life at large.

Keywords Community • Status group • Status markers • Collective goods • Social structure • Culture

© The Author(s) 2020
I. Rafanell, M. Sawicka, *Emotions in Digital Interactions*,
https://doi.org/10.1007/978-3-030-21998-7_5

The situated collective has been emphasized throughout the different sections presented in previous chapters as key to the emergence of social life in an intrinsic structuralist model. Individuals strive to belong to a collective by showing adherence to its internally held normative standards and avoiding negative evaluations from the members of the group of which they wish to be members. Barnes (1992) and Collins (2000, 2005) have extensively developed how groups operate as status groups; that is, as groups with defined boundaries characterized by sharing particular, internally held markers of honor and prestige. These groups are seen to exert a compelling force upon individuals' beliefs and practices via operating dynamics of exclusion and inclusion based on the possession or not of the group's status markers. These status markers should be seen as those which emerge from a community of practice, as already described. That is, status group markers are constitutive of the group boundaries as a community which shares a common language and concepts, a distinctive form or culture. In the empirical study we present, we will see how a newly embraced and redefined 'ethnopsychology' of motherhood becomes the distinctive status marker which will signal group membership. Individuals wishing to belong to a particular collective will demonstrate their willingness to belong by seeking the good opinion of the members only, and explicitly disregarding the opinions of outsiders as insignificant, flawed, or incorrect, or, in other words, as not providing any 'significant source of honor' (Barnes, 1992: 264). In doing so, individuals of a group constitute both the group and individual behavior.

Status group markers are status *symbols* which are conventional and very much situated. They are by nature fluid and changeable, and must be maintained and reinforced to ensure their existence and stability:

> The communicative purposes of status symbols are invaluable to smoothly operating everyday interactions [because] they are efficient indicators of how people are supposed to treat or be treated by others. Second, status symbols act as clear boundary markers, integrating those within the same status category while reifying the difference between those of different statuses. (Sauder, 2005: 281)

Sauder also notes that a shared conception of group status is key to a working consensus among members of a group. Thus, he emphasizes that a good understanding of group dynamics requires the elucidation of 'the micro-mechanics of status processes: how status is constituted, evidenced, maintained' (ibid., p. 282). To examine these mechanics is, Sauder concludes, key to understanding the meaning and consequences of status for the members of a group, and he highlights the 'acceptance or rejection of verbal claims' as a mechanism of granting or withdrawing status group markers.

When, as we have already noted, the existing frame of reference and linguistic categories of a community of origin do not allow for the expression of particular subjective experiences, individuals often seek commonality of experience in other quarters. Such migration frequently involves modifications to their pre-existing conceptual and linguistic frameworks, which are perceived as not adequate to reflect their personal experience. In such new environments, redefined descriptive linguistic categories emerge which, once they become collectively used, acquire an ontological grounding as 'reality' from the group members. Such redefined categories stand for objects and processes as 'collective goods, not individual properties' (Bloor, 1997: 14) and as such they become key identity signifiers of group membership, status group markers (Barnes, 1995: 135). Status markers are a new reality produced within a group in the process of group members sharing personal experiences, and in the process aligning their experiences with one another. Sauder adds that group markers as 'status symbols' are very much situated and are often contingent and fluid. As such, they must be continuously maintained. Moreover, their meaning is always contextual, so the same action or embodied marker acquires different meanings in different contexts (Sauder, 2005: 285).

Status group markers understood in this way emerge as the collective goods which define membership of the group and in doing so constitute its boundaries. Status group markers constitute both group membership and the group boundary, as well as the new linguistic and conceptual framework which will circulate among members of the group and facilitate successful interaction. Status markers emerge through interaction and act as communicative and relational tools without which the group would not be able to subsist. These status markers acting as group goods have another significant dimension: adopting them grants *distinctiveness* to the members belonging to the group, while failing to adopt them generates rejection and potential exclusion from the group. Losing access to the group and its group goods means losing those forms of social identity which are important to the group members, and with it the possibility of experiencing their own subjective experiences as real. The threat of membership exclusion acts as a reinforcement and reconstitution of the particular culture which is distinctive to the group as a community of shared knowledge and practice. Identifying the process by which such status markers emerge is key to understanding individual practice, group dynamics, and social life at large. In what follows, we show how newly redefined categories of motherhood become status group markers which constitute, as Barnes notes, collectively its reference. That is, they constitute a new reality intrinsic to that particular group.

BIBLIOGRAPHY

Barnes, B. (1992). Status Groups and Collective Action. *Sociology, 26*(2), 259–270.
Barnes, B. (1995). *The Elements of Social Theory*. London, UK: UCL Press.
Bloor, D. (1997). Collective Representations. In *Images and Reality*. Hungary: Hungarian Academy of Science.
Collins, R. (2000). Situational Stratification: A Micro-Macro theory of Inequality. *Social Theory, 18*(1), 17–43.
Collins, R. (2005). *Interaction Ritual Chains*. Princeton, NJ: Princeton University Press.
Sauder, M. (2005). Symbols and Contexts: An Interactionist Approach to the Study of Social Status. *The Sociological Quarterly, 46*(1), 279–298.

CHAPTER 6

Methodology and Methods of Data Collection

Abstract This chapter presents the methodological rationale for the empirical investigation presented in Part II. The core claim is that the analytical approach developed in the book requires a methodological focus on specific aspects of group dynamics, such as the inter-evaluative practices (methods) used by the members of a community to override heterogeneity and constitute consensus and social reality. Particular attention is given to three areas of social interactions within online bereavement communities of women after perinatal loss: how individual subjective accounts of the experience of perinatal loss are evaluated by other community members; how, because of this inter-evaluation dynamics, individuals modify their own accounts and align to the emerging group normative standards; which new linguistic categories emerge from the interactions and allow for the ontological grounding of—and thus legitimizing—the women's feelings of loss and grief. It also details the methods of data sourcing, and the approach adopted to data analysis based on a digital ethnography guided by the methodological focus developed as an intrinsic structuralist position.

Keywords Methodology • Qualitative methods • Digital ethnography • Digital sociology • Sociology of emotions • Qualitative content analysis (QCA)

© The Author(s) 2020
I. Rafanell, M. Sawicka, *Emotions in Digital Interactions*,
https://doi.org/10.1007/978-3-030-21998-7_6

The analytical approach developed in the previous part involves a methodological focus on specific aspects of group dynamics, namely the methods
used by members of a group in and through interaction which generate
consensus and the emergence of a new social reality. We develop this focus
by investigating three specific areas of social interaction. First, we pay
attention to individuals' subjective accounts of their experience of perinatal loss and, in particular, how they are evaluated by other members of the
online community within which they interact. Second, we observe, and
describe, how initial individual accounts are modified during these
exchanges, and highlight the tendency to align to other accounts advocated by other members of the group according to the evaluative judgments received. Third, we identify the new categories emerging and how
they become both strategic for grounding legitimacy to personal individual practice and feeling in relation to loss and grief, and key status group
markers signaling belonging and group membership.

As highlighted in the analytical section, a key method for the constitution of social life and group dynamics is affective sanctioning. In accordance with this, we identify how the members of these communities
sanction each other, paying particular attention to what negative and positive evaluative judgments they issue and how they transmit them.[1] In
doing so, we identify the constitutive nature of such dynamics of sanctioning by highlighting how they *norm* and *structure* the group dynamics and
identity. Here we chart the emergence of distinctive language and categories which facilitate communicative interaction, and a *shared* emotional
life-world, thus creating the normative standards to which it will be
expected that members of the group adjust. We also trace which new collective goods will emerge that will be used to mark the 'special' honor of
being a member of the group; that is, the 'objects' and personal attributes
which emerge as status markers. We consider how the new set of status
markers relates to the emerging emotional constellation of a redefined
experience of motherhood. With this, we also consider the particular
claims members make on outsiders, and the extent to which group formation in these cases may be a response to forms of negative pressure from
those branded as the outsiders. In doing so, we observe group formation
as the product of the process of distinguishing who belongs and who does

---

[1] For the development of these particular areas of focus we have taken inspiration from
Barnes' understanding of the key elements underpinning the formation of groups as status
groups (Barnes passim in the bibliography).

not vis-à-vis who partakes or not in this new emotional constellation. Lastly, we explore the process of embedding new linguistic categories and new contents within the group, by observing and describing how such status markers of membership facilitate emotional associations and attunement with one another, and a particular ethnopsychology of motherhood distinctive of the group's culture. We observe how these status markers result from group interactions in relation to who and what becomes legitimized, praised, silenced, and/or ostracized; that is, how the group status markers become and act as communicative tools, allowing members of the group to articulate and share particular subjective realizations of suffering, grieving, and sorrow. As the social constructionists we have discussed previously highlight, meaning construction is a mutual undertaking; that is, the capacity to collectively produce and recognize an adequate descriptive representation of individuals' subjective experience is key to individuals' membership of a collective (Heritage, 2008: 139).

6.1   DATA COLLECTION

Data utilized in this study were obtained from three major publicly available Polish online discussion lists for parents after perinatal loss. To our knowledge, in Poland at the time of the data collection there were only two such institutionalized associations of parents, and both were included in our research. Each of them has its own digital platform (where information, counseling materials, and medical advice are published, and useful links provided) and an open forum for users. The third data source was chosen based on its popularity measured by position in Google search results, which reflects the level of activity around a website. The underpinning methodological rationale for these choices was to identify and collect data from active, lively groups, organized around websites which, with a high level of probability, channel digital communication about miscarriage/stillbirth in Poland. As has already been indicated, our analytical approach is based on the assumption that social realities are generated through the micro-dynamics of social interaction; therefore, it was of the utmost importance that the threads selected to be included in the study offer a rich and dense network of communication.

From each of these sources one thread was chosen to be included in the analysis[2] based on the level of activity of users—following the rationale outlined earlier, the threads with the highest number of entries were selected. In the text that follows, we refer to our data sources as 'F1', 'F2', and 'F3'. F1 is a thread taken from a moderated forum of an association of parents who suffered perinatal loss. It revolves around the story of 'Jenny',[3] a young married woman. Her age can be deduced from the fact that at the moment of posting on the forum she was about to receive her bachelor's degree, which means she was about 22–23 years old, and her marital status from her mentioning of her husband's behaviors. Jenny suffered two consecutive miscarriages relatively early into her pregnancy, although based on the facts she discloses, it is difficult to state exactly in which weeks of her pregnancies the miscarriages took place. She initiated the thread by sharing her story, which is composed of three distinctive stages: her not wanting to get pregnant and being afraid of conceiving involuntarily; a transformation of the feelings she experienced; and her trying to conceive and finally conceiving successfully, but losing the first pregnancy. The thread continues when she receives responses from other users who also describe their stories, feelings, and thoughts, and on her part adds new details to the story of the first miscarriage and describes the second, which happened in the meantime.

F2, although not moderated, has a similar structure—it starts with a story of 'Kate', a young (about 26 years old based on her own declarations) married woman. Again, her marital status can be established based on her mentioning her husband, especially the fact that she is temporarily living apart from him due to his professional obligations in Sweden. Kate suffered a stillbirth—her son was burdened with a lethal defect and was born dead in the 39th week of pregnancy. Although she was informed about the defect in the 24th week of pregnancy, she decided not to terminate. The thread revolves around her expressing her feelings and thoughts, and posting messages addressed to the lost son, which form a narrative of her loss. This narrative is complemented with entries by other users who also share their stories.

[2] For ethical reasons we do not provide links to the data sources. Although being able to access the original data would probably enable readers to make their own observations, we are convinced that in the case of a scientific investigation into sensitive experiences, the priority is to protect the identities of the individuals whose experiences are considered.

[3] We do not provide the users' real names or nicknames. The names given in the text that follows are pseudonyms that we invented for each individual we quote.

Table 6.1 Characteristic of the data sources

Source number	Moderation	Anchoring entry (protagonist)
F1	Yes	Yes
F2	No	Yes
F3	No	No

F3 is structured differently. It is not an online forum *sensu stricto*, but a commentary section under an entry on the blog of a midwife who writes in general terms and from a professional perspective about miscarriage. Under this entry other users (readers of the blog) share their stories, thoughts, and feelings connected to their personal experiences of miscarriages and communicate with each other. This means that in contrast to F1 and F2, F3 is not anchored in any leading story, nor does it have an individual protagonist (in the case of F1 it is Jenny who is the protagonist, in case of F2 Kate). Unlike F1, F3 is not moderated.

A simplified characteristic of the data sources may be presented as in Table 6.1.

By selecting the data sources just mentioned, we included in the analysis threads differing in the extent to which they are structured by default settings and formal solutions adopted by a platform which mediates communication. F1 is the most structured, being both moderated and anchored in an entry written by a protagonist of the thread; F2 is less structured, as it is not moderated but is still anchored in an entry by a protagonist; F3 is the least structured, because it is neither moderated nor anchored in a protagonist's entry.

In this sense, we accessed groups of three different formats, as each of these factors (moderation and anchoring in an individual story) significantly influences the dynamics of communication in the group. We aimed at diversifying communication formats by choosing differently structured groups in order to ensure a comprehensive overview of digital interaction dynamics. The qualitative features of the data sources and their volume—in sum providing more than 1000 individual entries[4]—enabled us to achieve theoretical saturation and address research questions.

Additionally, interviews with three moderators of F1 were conducted. In this case, the moderators are recruited through an informal procedure

---

[4] F1 was composed of 479 individual entries, F2 of 492 entries, F3 of 374 entries.

from long-term users of the discussion list. Essentially, already active moderators invite individuals who in their view are exceptionally polite and kind towards other users to join them in the task of moderating the forum. Due to this, we assumed that the moderators would be able to provide the insider's perspective on the interactions ongoing within this particular bereavement community. The interviews were carried out before the content analysis of the digital communication, with the aim of collecting initial guiding data to aid in the design of the coding categories to be used in the analysis. As we perceived the moderators mainly as individuals with the experience of perinatal loss, we assumed that the emerging framework of analytical concepts stemming from the interviews may be also applied to data collected in other groups. However, the reviews resulted in a rich source of data more important than only contextual, and were included in the actual data set. For ethical reasons we decided not to contact women who were individual users of the analyzed forums.[5] Due to this, no interviews were conducted with members of F2. As F3 had no official moderator, the interview conducted with the owner of this forum was not included in the data set.

6.2   Data Analysis

The process of analytical investigation into the data was composed of three phases. Firstly, the data was read and coded for emerging patterns following an integrated thematic analysis approach. Thematic analysis is defined as a method for 'identifying, analyzing and reporting patterns (themes) within data' (Braun and Clarke, 2006: 79). The advantage of this method is its relative openness—it could be adopted to various theoretical frameworks, and it 'can be a method that works both to reflect reality and to unpick or unravel the surface of "reality"' (p. 81), which makes it especially suitable and adequate for the aims of our study. The main analytical choice that must be decided upon when using a thematic analysis approach is what should be treated as a 'theme' emerging from the data. In an

[5] We assume that there is an important difference between individual users of the forums and individuals who agree to become moderators. The latter are also informal representatives and 'spokespersons' of their group. This assumption was confirmed by the interviewees themselves; in the interviews they stated that it was important for them to participate in both research about miscarriage and media campaigns on this topic, because their organization aims at broadening public consciousness of the emotional experiences of parents who have suffered perinatal loss.

admittedly broad answer to this issue, Braun and Clarke note: '[A] theme captures something important about the data in relation to the research question, and represents some level of patterned response or meaning within a data set' (p. 82).

For this reason, in the second stage of the analysis, the original analytical framework presented in Part I of this volume was applied to the data set, and the coding structure was developed. The application of a specific analytical framework enabled us to identify key themes in the data set; that is, to capture—paraphrasing Braun and Clarke—what is important about the data and which patterns are *the* patterns that matter. In tune with the analytical framework we developed, in the analysis we focused on the communicative interactions related to the areas of practice already delineated: sanctioning, norming, structuring, and embedding. These, therefore, would point at the methods individuals used, which would act as the organizing principles of social interactions and would underpin the social reality which would ensue from them. These were clearly patterned around the following themes:

1. Feelings of exclusion from the participants' social environment of origin based on the negation of their experience of loss and grief.
2. Efforts made among the members of the group to ontologically ground their experience of loss and grief.
3. Finally, the emergence of new social phenomena, such as a new reality of the unborn, and a redefinition of motherhood under the category of Angel's motherhood.

During this stage of the analysis, we refined the coding structure, and compared and contrasted themes identified across the data set, revealing key themes and locating them within the data set.

Thirdly, we conducted in-depth micro-analysis within the theme of affective sanctioning—we considered all the identified instances of sanctioning as it occurred among the users of the forums in their exchanges. At this stage, the focus was on interaction, actions (entries), and reactions (entries posted in reply). We aimed at investigating what was going on *between* individuals who engage in sanctioning, and, in this way, revealing key aspects of the micro-interactional dynamics through which a new social reality emerges, and which will circumscribe the emotional experiences of those members of a community of interactants.

BIBLIOGRAPHY

Braun, V., & Clarke, V. (2006). Using Thematic Analysis in Psychology. *Qualitative Research in Psychology, 3*(2), 77–101.

Heritage, J. (2008 [1984]). *Garfinkel and Ethnomethodology.* Cambridge, UK: Polity Press.

PART II

The Emergence of a New Ethnopsychology of Motherhood

CHAPTER 7

Emotional Deviance and New Emotional Reality

Abstract This chapter presents the results of the empirical investigation into online bereavement communities of women who suffered perinatal loss. It reveals interactional mechanisms underlying the process of identity loss, and the search for ontological groundings of new social identity. Identity loss is triggered by exclusionary practices from the women's communities of origin—which, in turn, are experienced as negating the reality of their grieving and their right to experience, and manifest, suffering. Consequently, these women are compelled to search for new communities where their experiences are recognized, and a new identity corresponding with their feelings is reclaimed. This new membership, it is argued, allows for their suffering to obtain an ontologically grounded status of reality which legitimizes their emotional suffering. The data reveals how, during digital interactions, the women joining these online groups undergo dynamics of inter-evaluative practices via affective sanctioning mechanisms which generate an inter-alignment of their differing subjective accounts of perinatal loss. This results in the establishment of a new conception of motherhood signified by the emergence of the categories of Angel baby and Angels' mother. Around these categories an emotional 'life-world' develops as a new ethnopsychology of motherhood, idiosyncratic to these online communities.

Keywords Online bereavement communities • Digital ethnography • Digital sociology • Affective sanctioning • Ethnopsychology • Grief

© The Author(s) 2020   63
I. Rafanell, M. Sawicka, *Emotions in Digital Interactions*,
https://doi.org/10.1007/978-3-030-21998-7_7

In the dominant European emotional culture, miscarriage and stillbirth are culturally perceived as events on the verge of 'real' death (see James, 2000; Hazen, 2003; Keefe-Cooperman, 2004 [2005]; Lang et al., 2011). As such, they bring about particular social and emotional consequences for those who experience them and, through them, individuals enter into a social void: they lose newly acquired identity of mothers, but are given no clear cultural alternative (Sawicka, 2017). Thus, miscarriage and still-birth frequently result in the rise of emotions experienced by the bereaved individuals as 'ambiguous' or 'disenfranchised' (Lang et al., 2011; Sawicka, 2017). In the present investigation, we claim that such emotions should be seen as indicators of the micro-social processes key to reality formation and the ordering of group dynamics: what is experienced as an identity loss is triggered by certain exclusionary practices that bereaved women experience from significant others in their communities of origin. These exclusionary practices are experienced as negating the reality of their loss and grief, and, consequently, their right to experience and manifest loss and grief. Subsequently, they are compelled to search for an interactional context in which an identity corresponding with their feelings may be reclaimed, allowing their suffering to obtain an ontologically grounded reality which legitimizes the emotional suffering they undergo. Online bereavement communities can be regarded as such a context: during computer-mediated interactions within a web-based bereavement community, an alternative identity is elaborated and established. As a result, a new social reality emerges: an ethnopsychology of Angel motherhood, which serves as a repertoire of cultural means to guide emotions accompanying miscarriage or stillbirth, and invest them with meaning.

In the sections that follow, we reveal interactional mechanisms which underlie the process of identity loss, identity reclaim, and its ontological grounding, as it occurs in and through discursive interactions in which the bereaved women participate.

7.1   Exclusionary Practices: Negating Loss and Grief

Although the women who join online bereavement communities are het-erogeneous insofar as they come from different social backgrounds and are of different ages and levels of education,[1] a distinctive shared feature of

---

[1]According to our interviewees, moderators, and long-term users of the forum. Additionally, the heterogeneity of the users of non-moderated forums can be deduced from occasional remarks pertaining to their socioeconomic situation: the users sometimes disclose

the members of these online communities is that they have been subjected to affective sanctioning in the form of negative evaluations from members within their context of origin, vis-à-vis their right or, to be more precise, lack of the right to experience grief or loss. In this sense, the members of these online communities emerged from a shared initial experience of *exclusionary* practices. Their accounts vary in the form which these exclusionary practices took, but not in the content: they offer descriptions of different verbal and non-verbal expressions of the same experienced rejection received towards their emotional experience of loss and grief. Based on their accounts, different types of the general theme of exclusionary practices can be reconstructed. The bereaved women recall:

> our befriended priests prayed for us when I told them about the next pregnancy, one of them even celebrated a thanksgiving mass. When I texted them though (I am still not able to make phone calls) to say that another Baby is gone, none of them answered... *[Jenny, F1]*

and:

> Friends often visit me, but they usually talk only about themselves, and they don't even mention my son, and when I mention him, they just say that it was God's will and they cut short this topic. *[Kate, F2]*

In these quotes, the women recall a type of affective sanctioning which takes the form of *silencing* practices. Silencing comprises actions such as cutting short a conversation in which the lost baby is mentioned, avoiding this topic in a conversation, or changing the topic when the lost baby is mentioned. All such reactions of significant others (family, friends, or authority figures such as priests) inform the bereaved women that their case—the situation of a perinatal loss—constitutes a kind of social 'taboo' (Sawicka, 2017). By silencing the emotions and the subjective experiences of these women, their close peers effectively withdraw the possibility of referring to the experience. If referring acts have to be understood as key constitutive elements of the reality of social life, then the silencing of a woman's experience in the form of denying her voice is highly significant, as it effectively makes such experiences become not real, foreclos-

information about their age, occupation, or place of residence, which proves that very different individuals actually suffer because of miscarriage or stillbirth and enter the forums to share their stories.

ing, as a consequence, any existential grounding to her subjectively lived emotional pain. As Barnes notes, what constitute social life are acts of reference and self-reference *of a community* of individuals. Therefore, when the community silences a particular individual experience, what is effectively being done is the withdrawal of the right of such experiences to exist, leaving these individuals in a social limbo, where personal experience acquires an ambiguous and undefined sense of reality. Individuals in this case may end up even doubting the authenticity of their own emotional pain, generating manifold negative sentiments of self-worth and self-doubt.

Another set of exclusionary practices described involves actions through which others surrounding the bereaved define their loss as insignificant. Kate describes the following experience:

> People around me tell me that I had time to get accustomed to this thought *[that her baby will not be born alive]*, because I'd known since the 24th week about the lethal defect, but how can you get accustomed to the thought that your child is going to die, how?? *[Kate, F2]*

A loss expected is framed by interactional partners of the woman talking here as a loss less acute or less significant, or even less real. The downscaling of the experience of loss, and therefore the right to grief, is a common experience shared by online community members:

> I'm fed up with these 'consolations' like 'you're young, you'll have another one' or 'but you haven't even seen the baby'. *[Mary, F3]*

> the nurse said 'stop crying, you'll have another baby, you're young' *(...)*. When we went to a cemetery to light two candles, my mother in-law asked 'but for whom?' *[Sally, F3]*

> Slogans like 'it happens so often nowadays'/'you'll surely succeed next time'/'everything's going to be all right' make me want to cry out loud that all I want is to be left alone. *[Angela, F3]*

Such framing sharply contrasts with previous categorizations of pregnancy that these women receive before the loss, which unambiguously show acknowledgment of the existence of the unborn baby. The withdrawal of such existence when suffering perinatal loss is acutely experienced as illogical by the women of the online communities, opening up the potential for redefinition, which will take place in the forums, as to what should to be taken to be motherhood and babyhood. This contrast is revealed by a long-term user of forum F1, when during an interview she says:

It is like that, you get pregnant and everyone is happy, the grandparents are delighted etc. And then you lose the pregnancy and you feel as if it had never been there, nobody says anything; before that, there was a baby, there were questions, 'do you feel that it will be a boy or a girl?' and so on, and after that: 'come on, it wasn't a baby yet.' *[Interview no. 2]*

By pointing to the fact that the fetus was laden with a lethal defect (or any defect), or lost at an early stage of pregnancy, the others surrounding the bereaved engage in *lessening* practices through which the importance of loss is diminished and minimized. When the fetus is categorized as 'not a baby yet' or 'a defected baby', it is also framed as too minor a reason to be the source of a legitimate long-lasting sorrow. This is a clear example of another type of silencing of these women's experience of grief and loss, which takes a form of what could be defined as an ontological demotion of the status of babyhood. The last quote is a perfect exemplification of the fluid and open-ended nature of category ascription and content, which we refer to previously as the nature of all category ascription. As the content of the referring category is never fully determined and fixed in any context, it allows for both the lessening redefinitions of the pain of women experiencing perinatal loss by others in their communities of origin, and also for the redefinitions produced by the women within these online communities. As we will see later, these women will actively engage in the construction of new categories, with new redefined content more appropriate to ground and describe their lived experience of loss and grief.

A third category of exclusionary practices identified in these women's accounts was the negative sanctioning of the emotional display of their grief and sorrow:

Rose: Unfortunately, my mum is also tactless ... Just recently I have been looking through the window and there was a mother with a stroller, I begun to shed tears again, and my mum reacted: 'come on, stop it, you'll walk with your stroller too' ... Is it so hard to understand *[for others]* that this is an immense suffering *(...)*

Kate: Yes, *(...)*, they *[i.e. outsiders to the group]* can hardly understand that *(...)* we are left with this terrible longing and pain :(*[F2]*

and:

Everyone around me tells me that I have to get back to normality, but, hell with it, there's nothing I have to, I don't want to! *[Alice, F2]*

> Just recently I have been stopped in the street by a woman I know and she said: '*[Kate]* you have to stop going over it, you have to start living, it was meant to be that way' *[Kate, F2]*

That such remarks are perceived as a type of, painfully experienced, negative sanctioning is proven by the emotions they elicit in the bereaved women: anger, irritation, and a sense of rejection, all of which surface in the following exchange on F2 between Kate and Rose. Lack of empathy and sympathy are experienced as a deeply unfair chastisement which elicits angry reactions at not being 'understood'. When Kate reveals that some people tell her that she had time to 'get accustomed' to the idea that she would not be able to give birth successfully, as she was informed in the 24th week of pregnancy that her baby had a lethal chromosomal defect, Rose is incensed:

> If somebody told me that I had time to get accustomed to the thought about child's death I would physically attack this person ... How can you say such a thing! That's another proof that if someone didn't experience it, they shouldn't say anything at all!

In such interactions, we can see how the internal validation of the experiences of these women in the online communities operates. Not only do they share and acknowledge the pain of the other women, but they use emotionally loaded, negative evaluations of the reactions these women have received from significant others in their communities of origin. In doing so, they construct the outsider and the insider, and those who 'understand' and those who do not, therefore devaluing the opinions of the outsiders, and facilitating communicative interaction among themselves as members of the group.

The interviewees corroborate that the denial of the reality of loss from members of their community of origin appears to be the fundamental experience of all women who join the forums, one that brings them together and prompts them to share their stories in search of compassion and understanding. Empathy is one of the most powerful ways to demonstrate an affective positive sanctioning and one that clearly signals the honoring of the experiences of the other members of these forums:

> They *[users]* often repeat to each other 'I know what you feel, I understand you perfectly well', 'nobody will understand you, only here you'll find compassion', 'we here understand each other very well, people around will never understand us'. They repeat that over and over again. *[Interview no. 1]*

I was lucky enough to have a husband who supported me and parents who showed understanding, but there are women who don't have anyone ... Even the husbands expect that they start behaving normally *(...)* so the women can write what they feel only on the forum, crying secretly in front of the screen when the husband does not see. *[Interview no. 2]*

These instances of negatively sanctioning the emotional display of saying sorry as impulsive and untoward constitute a set of *norming* practices, through which the individuals surrounding the bereaved women attempt to bring them in line with feeling norms rooted in dominant emotional culture of their society. Indeed, the deference emotion system displayed here is one in which there is a prescription, as it were, of obligatory happiness. This excludes de facto any right to mourn, and therefore attempting to bring into line the feelings and emotions of these women thus reinforcing the currently practiced and accepted emotional frame of reference of the dominant ethnopsychology. Sadness and depression are seen as deviant to the norm and thus to the group at large. The demand made to these women to display 'proper' feelings, by deeming their emotional outbursts as 'ostentations' and 'improper', is a form of shaming which discredits the subjective experiences of these women. This is framed as an obligation towards their social peers: it takes a shape of a feeling norm, which bans sadness as it is supposed to negatively influence the moods of the people around these women. The display of sadness and grief is framed as a threat to other people's emotional well-being in particular, and as a general threat to the well-being of the community. As one of the users puts it:

they *[others]* say so *[=that the user will get pregnant again]*, because they want to get back to normality, and they want to treat you as if nothing had happened. They want to live on. The people around me want that as well. *[Kate, F2]*

Silencing, lessening, and qualifications of impropriety are *norming* practices towards the dominant feeling norm existing in their communities. Because the dominant feeling norm applied to bereaved women is one which carries an important constitutive self-referential component of what ought to be taken as real, the imperative that these women should stop mourning their loss embodies a particular definition of motherhood in which their experience is not included. In other words, the message conveyed by such exclusionary mechanisms is performative, that is, constitutive in nature: in implying that there is no reason to mourn as they have not been mothers yet, the community re-establishes what is to be taken as motherhood and what is not. Furthermore, this is a protection of the existing feeling norms which results in a further ontological grounding as 'commonsensical' of the existing conventions of the particular ethnopsychology of these communities.

By the same token, through these norming practices, the bereaved women's subjective experience is denied recognition—they lose their previously granted social status of mothers and, perhaps even more significantly, their suffering loses ontological status. As a result, they are 'made' de facto outsiders in the social context in which they live as 'emotional deviants'.[2] The intensity with which this exclusion is felt is exemplified by how one of the interviewees describes and characterizes the reactions of unsympathetic others:

> hey, you are all lunatics (...) You seal up in your pain, what on Earth is going on here on this forum, it's madness, mental hospital, get back to reality. *[Interview no. 1]*

Members of these bereavement communities are very self-aware of how they are being negatively sanctioned. They are acutely aware that they are not only stripped of their feelings, but also of their rationality altogether. Accusations of madness are typically encountered when individuals threaten the order of the group, in this case the order generated by the collective adherence to a shared and accepted ethnopsychology of motherhood. Such practices of exclusions carry a heavy price, as the loneliness experienced is also a derivative of a loss of the social self:

> Kate: People around me prefer to pretend that they don't see my pain, and that everything is fine with me, as two months have gone by *[i.e. since stillbirth]*, and that's why I hardly ever go out and I don't meet with anyone because I'm not able to pretend *[that everything is alright]*...

> Rose: Neither do I have anyone to talk about what I feel, I even don't want to, because I know that no-one will understand ... Only here on this forum I find consolation, only you—Angels' Mothers know how to help me... *[F2]*

---

[2] We refer here to the concept of 'emotional deviance' introduced to the sociology of emotions by Thoits (1990).

We begin to see clearly here how a new community is being constituted by the identification of who belongs (the forum members who
share similar experiences and sympathies), and by framing the other as
'those people who do not understand' and whose opinion is disregarded
as unworthy. Avoiding interaction with such 'others' is a self-exclusionary
practice, used to internally devalue the significance of the opinions of
these others.

All these different types of exclusionary practices will underpin and
shape a new world of perception, a new perspective which will become the
basis for the construction of a new community of belonging, based on the
mutual recognition of shared experience. Exclusionary practices make
these women feel lonely in a distinctive way which they all share, and the
purposeful identification and accounting of the commonality of this particular subjective experience create such loneliness as one of the group's
status markers. A reflexive account of this experience, and how it homog-
enizes an otherwise heterogeneous set of individuals, is provided by a
moderator of F1, who states:

> I think that all of us feel to some extent lonely. Maybe it is so that everyone
> is lonely in suffering, but, as I say, these are all people *[i.e. users]* who are …
> Yes, I think it is a good word, lonely. Not because they don't have friends
> and relatives around them, they do have, but in the way they go through
> their loss they feel lonely. And this is the only thing that I see *[that the users
> have in common]*, because the rest—these are all different stories, and *[mis-
> carriage happens]* in different life circumstances, and different people write
> about this. And there is this feeling … This feeling of loneliness appears,
> because it *[i.e. miscarriage]* is taboo, right? Taboo in the sense that no one
> talks about it, right? During family get-together no one mentions it, our
> babies *[=lost]* don't form part of our family history. *[Interview no. 4]*

These women experience the exclusion, silencing, and minimizing of
their grief to such an extent that they feel like the outsiders in their own
communities. It is not the experience of miscarriage and suffering per se
that they share in these exchanges, but rather the loss of the existential
grounding granted, and available, to full members of their community.
Sharing their experience of feeling excluded with other women with whom
they can inter-subjectively identify opens up the possibility to legitimize
their own individual experiences, and to validate, and partake in, further
self-exclusionary practices. In these particular cases, *self*-exclusion is redefined in ways which allow them to legitimize their subjective experience of
grief by the constitution of a new group to which they can feel they belong.

The construction of such group belonging, allowing these women to inter-subjectively communicate their own experience with other women who ratify their feelings, also generates the validation of these experiences, normalizing them and accordingly becoming the accepted standard of feeling norms for the whole community. Once such feelings become the property of the community, they become part and parcel of their linguistic repertoire and will therefore allow for an array of self-referring instances which, following Barnes, will constitute the reality of the object to which they make reference—in this particular case, the authenticity of their own suffering and pain. This results in the necessary ontological grounding of their own experience to become a guiding principle for practice. For instance, it affords them the right to refuse to comply with the demands of unsympathetic others, and to engage in practices of self-exclusion as Alice, an F2 user, claims:

> everyone around me tells me that I have to get back to normality, but, hell with it, there's nothing I have to, I don't want to! *[Alice, F2]*

Constituting themselves as a community through the validation which results from the sharing, recognition, mutual endorsement, and ratification of their lived emotional experience is key to being able to contest and challenge the existing feeling norms of their communities of origin, which they consider unfair and unjust. These women show particular resistance to these silencing and exclusionary practices towards their strongly felt subjective emotional experiences, because they perceive it as a demotion of their social status and value within their communities. When family members and friends are labeled as 'those who do not understand' and as the 'others', their disapproval can be rejected as illegitimate and help to compensate for the loss of social standing the group members experience. In this way the women constitute group membership by identifying the particular aspect which outsiders do not possess—namely, that particular experience of loss and grief which only they can understand—and, as such, this feeling becomes a key group status marker by which all members of the community must abide. These bereaved women, rather than accepting and aligning the feeling norms of their communities of origin, which would mean abandoning or redefining their experience of suffering, seek other contexts where they can find individuals with whom they can share and validate their experience. Such an opportunity is offered by these web-based communities for parents who have suffered perinatal loss. If feelings of loneliness, exclusion, or silencing are what unite them and compel them to join these forums, once they enter these communities they inevitably engage in the group forming and maintenance dynamics inherent in all group formation. To this we turn our attention in the next section.

7.2   New Linguistic Categories: Redefining Motherhood

As already noted, the individuals who join these online forums are hetero- geneous in many ways. Joining the group and becoming a participant entail a process of mutual adjustment of their individually varying experi- ences. Group formation involves the alignment of all members of the group to the internally held norms, beliefs, and practices. These, in turn, become the group's significant status markers. It is essential that the group generates a shared frame of reference, enhancing communicative interac- tion in order to achieve consensus and alignment. In this process, indi- viduals engage in creating new, or redefining their existing repertoire of, linguistic categories and labels which can be used to meaningfully express their experience. In order for these redefinitions to succeed in becoming the group's commonly accepted stock of knowledge and norms, individu- als must engage in a process of inter-subjective interaction, from where consensus must emerge. As Barnes and Scheff note, a key mechanism underpinning the generation of consensus and agreement among differing individuals is the use of affective sanctions in the form of a deference- emotion system. This process is clearly visible in of the dynamics of inter- actions within the online bereavement communities we investigated. In what follows, we identify the different forms of affective sanctioning exer- cised *within the group*, which result in the delineation of new categories and the constitution of the new form of ethnopsychology which is shared by members of this group.

The analysis of the accounts of the bereaved women—primarily of their references to the experience of loneliness—makes clear that they join the online communities seeking to validate their subjective experiences. This validation takes place when they realize that their experience is reflected in the experience of many others in the group. As Barnes notes, individuals checking with others is a key mechanism to confirm the correctness and plausibility of one's experience. This is plainly illustrated by the following remark from one of the interviewees:

one enters *[the forum]* and sees tens, hundreds of stories of women who mourn their babies, and thinks 'oh, so I'm not crazy after all'. *[Interview no. 2]*

The realization that other individuals have a similar experience of loss and grief provides a social context in which feelings deemed as irrational in their communities of origin, and therefore illegitimate, are given the social recognition of rationality, and can thus be legitimately publicly voiced.

This initial recognition of a shared experience does not automatically produce consensus, however. Analysis of interactive exchanges ongoing within the communities shows that the members joining the online forums are heterogeneous in many ways. Long-term users of the forums also note that, based on their experience, it would be very difficult to pinpoint what the users have in common prior to entering the forums:

> very different women come here *(...)* highly educated, and young, rather simple girls ... From big cities and from small villages... *[Interview no. 2]*

> These are *(...)* all people, for whom miscarriage was a tragedy. *(...)* If there is something more we have in common, I don't know, I don't see any such thing. *[Interview no. 4]*

This heterogeneity makes it inevitable that the women who enter the group will bring differing views and voices. As stressed earlier, a community constitutes its boundaries by generating a shared symbolic linguistic apparatus which overrides differing practices and views. This commonly shared stock of knowledge and practice emerges from the inter-alignment of the members of the group, generated by the internal use of sanctioning mechanisms. Much like in everyday interactions of communities at large, these online forums operationalize positive and negative evaluative sanctioning, in the form of honoring (priding) and dishonoring (shaming) of those members seen as agreeing with, or deviating from, the internally embraced narratives and feeling norms associated with the experience of perinatal loss. In doing so, these communities of women construct and establish the reality, intrinsic to the group, of their loss and grief. The different sections we develop in what follows aim to show the process of generation of a new category of motherhood, which emerges from these online communities. It also aims to demonstrate how these communities constitute a new reality, such as a redefined new category of motherhood, which allows them to ontologically ground their subjective lived experience negated in the outside world.

This redefined idea of motherhood is grounded in specific aspects of their experience, and takes the form of delineating particular experiences and categories as key signifiers of the newly adopted categorization of motherhood. These are in particular the redefinition and legitimation of the nature of their suffering and the redefinition of the reality of baby-hood. In turn, these two aspects acquire the status of key signifiers of status group markers, and have a key role in the constitution of the category of motherhood shared by the members of these communities.

7.2.1 Reclaiming Loss and Grief as a Collective Good

Expressing and sharing the personal experience of pain and suffering forms the key aspect of the interactive exchanges taking place in these forums. These accounts, however, are constantly monitored by other members of the community. Through micro-analysis of extracts from their conversations, we can identify the methods used in such monitoring, which take the form of an ever-present evaluative, affective sanctioning exercised among members of these communities. In analyzing such exchanges, we can identify the sets of feelings which are fostered and supported, and the ones which are suppressed and disapproved of. In these exchanges we see not only a corroboration of others' feelings, but also how these feelings are made to conform with the overall narrative maintained in the group vis-à-vis their internally held ethnopsychology of feeling norms. In other words, the members of these communities not only seek to confirm their own personal experience but also, in doing so, modify it according to how others react to their accounts. The following passages demonstrate this process of negotiation of their own experience of suffering after their losses, and of feeling norms regarding the experience of regret and dismay. Kate expresses her pain after stillbirth:

> It is so terrible to feel you are a mum, and not to be able to hug your baby … (…) I don't understand why God gives us such a tiny being to take it away so abruptly, so that it can't even cry, like my son couldn't … Oh, it hurts so much… :(:(*[Kate, F2]*

Among a variety of straightforward sympathetic and comforting replies, she also receives the following reply which contains a different account of the experience of loss and, included in it, a suggestion of how Kate should modify her own experience:

> *[Your son]* decided to be with you for all this time *[i.e. period of pregnancy before stillbirth]* and this is something you should be grateful for. You had the chance to feel his moves, and not all the Angels' Mothers have such a chance (…). *[Caroline, F2]*

We can see how this other user's response to Kate initiates the process of a redefinition of the experience of loss, by displaying a subtle but clear negative evaluation of Kate's account of her experience. With the injunction 'you should be grateful', Caroline negatively evaluates Kate's own experience, clearly chastising her for her lack of acknowledgment of the 'privilege' she had, over other members of this community, through being able to feel the fetus. In doing so, it provides the basis for a new feeling norm to be used to regulate emotional experiences deriving from a perinatal loss, one that redefines the suffering as a privilege (and therefore something to be happy about) rather than something to be angry and feel despondent about. Furthermore, by ascribing wide agency and high status to Kate's stillborn son (Kate's son is seen as 'deciding to be' with Kate for that long, and no shorter or longer), Caroline simultaneously redefines the category of baby. This is not a fetus, but a baby in its own right, with an unquestionable capacity for choice and agency, and which should be conceived as more important than Kate's personal pain. This can be regarded as a clear instance of *shaming*. Caroline implies that Kate, by putting so much emphasis on her loss and her pain, in fact undervalues the existence of her son. Shaming serves here as a method of silencing the feelings which do not comply or coincide with the internally held ethnopsychology and feeling rules of this community. As a result, a new set of proper and correct feelings are being redefined and constituted, which take the form of transforming the feeling of pain into gratitude. Kate reacts to this in the following way:

> It doesn't matter how long they *[i.e. lost babies]* have been with us, the pain is always immense. But you are right, I could hold him for a moment in my arms, and not all the Angels' Mothers had the chance to have such an experience... *[Kate, F2]*

Kate engages in two operations here. On the one hand, she engages in self-management of the loss of face generated by Caroline's chastising remarks by further emphasizing the personal experience of pain, regardless of the length of pregnancy time, and thus its legitimacy. On the other hand, we clearly see the effective results of Caroline's sanctioning in how Kate starts redefining her own experience, realigning it with the new frame of reference of feeling proposed by Caroline. In this new frame of reference, the high status ascribed to the unborn baby demands feelings of gratitude for any type of contact with them, however short this may be. In this interaction, and through shaming and negatively evaluating Kate's feelings, Caroline instates a new feeling norm, one which demotes personal experience of sadness and pain as a key signifier and grants it to the baby. We will see how the granting of a higher status to the baby, over and above Kate's personal feelings, will be key to generating an internal redefinition of motherhood.

This negotiation between the right to grieve and yet to be happy for having been able to be with the unborn baby, however short the time, is common in another of the forums analyzed. Jenny expresses her general regret for all babies lost, and the suffering it brings about:

> This was not supposed to be this way ... Why so many stories do not end with a happy ending? Why in our case each fairy-tale turn into a drama? (...) The only thing that's left from my Neverland are two good Spirits *[i.e. two babies lost through miscarriage]* who I miss so much! *[Jenny, F1]*

She receives the following reply from another user, who supports her account and further emphasizes the legitimacy of the pain by noting that she would have preferred not to have experienced this loss:

> Unfortunately, for us a different screenplay was written, our story won't end with a happy ending, and we can't change it. I think that each of us would like to live in a different fairy-tale. *[Daisy, F1]*

To this, Jenny reacts in an unexpected way, but one which coincides with what Caroline also did, by granting high status to the unborn babies via recognizing their real existence:

> *[Daisy]*, I do not want a different fairy-tale, because a different fairy-tale would be without my Little One and my Bubble. True, maybe there would have been other kids, but I so desperately wanted them, these kids, not other kids! *[Jenny, F1]*

This response can again be regarded as another instance of shaming, where Jenny negatively sanctions Daisy for regretting having lived through the experience of miscarriage. We see that this is clearly felt as an instance of shaming when we consider Daisy's reaction:

> I do feel that I would like to tear out some pages from this like-a-fairy-tale. I won't say it's easy, because it's not. I won't pretend it's all right, because it's not. I don't need to explain this, you're going through the same thing. *[Daisy, F1]*

Daisy engages in attempts to circumvent the shaming exercised by Jenny by implying that Jenny 'is pretending', whereas she herself is sincere, or authentic—she states that she 'won't pretend'. By implying that Jenny should examine her feelings more closely—'I don't need to explain this, you're going through the same thing'—she also includes a reference to a community of shared feelings. Pointing to the fact that they share the same feelings allows her to place herself on the same 'side' as Jenny, within the 'we' group. This reaction may be regarded as another attempt to avoid the attribution of shame—hitherto shaming exercises were directed primarily at individuals from outside the community, as 'those who do not understand' feelings accompanying a perinatal loss. Reinstating the legitimacy of the experience of pain is key to the formation of the collective to which the bereaved women aim to belong, so it is something which will be heavily protected, and one of the reasons women join these forums. However, what we see in these instances is how the feeling norms being constituted are open-ended and fluid in nature, and constantly negotiated even though they are anchored in a clear starting point: the need to feel validated in one's own experience of pain. What we observe here is how the members of this community negotiate two aspects which become key signifiers of group belonging, on the one hand the right to suffer and on the other the reality of the baby—which implies some downgrading of the right to suffer, but in particular that of regret. This generates some tension, which engages the members of these communities in a plethora of interactive accounts, where we can see the processes of definition and redefinition of the content and meaning of feeling rules emerging.

For example, further instances of this process of suppression of the experience of regret, through discrediting any expressions of rejection of the experience of loss, is also visible in a parallel conversation between Jenny and another user of F1, Greta. Greta rejects her situation and expresses her regret, stating to 'hell with such a plan'; that is, this situation or course of life. Jenny reacts:

> [Greta]—maybe in fact not, maybe because what we've gone through, we are stronger, more emphatic, more tender, and we will appreciate what we have more (...). I don't regret any moment of pregnancy, any minute of it—starting from the positive test result, through the pain, hemorrhage, falling hcg levels, and hemorrhage again (...). Would I like to be able to turn back time? Sure, I would like to be in hospital now, waiting for my Little One. Do I want to have living babies? Sure, I do, but (...) not instead of the Little One and the Bubble—they were too wonderful to stay here with me, created for Heaven. [Jenny, F1]

Once again, Jenny uses the same narrative as Caroline above in censuring Greta for showing regret; that is, the emphasis on the reality and the high status of the unborn babies. In this entry, Jenny also engages in another form of negative affective sanctioning towards Greta by displaying a form of shaming, through verbalizing a very descriptive portraiture of her physical suffering connected to pregnancy loss. Her detailed medical description of the process of miscarriage and the physical pain suffered has the function of strengthening her position, that despite the suffering she does not regret the experience and, although not directly expressed, the implication of this comment is that nor should Greta. To this, Greta reacts by producing a new account which realigns her with this feeling norm:

Neither do I regret the time spent with my Crumble *[the time of pregnancy]*... But letting go is so difficult... *[Greta, F1]*

This realignment implies accepting the new hierarchy of values articulated here; that is, the assumption that the opportunity (framed as a privilege) to be with the unborn babies, for whatever amount of time, outweighs the psychological and physical suffering deriving from the loss. As a result, a feeling norm which fosters gratitude and discourages regret emerges, as is underlined by Jenny again in her next entry:

I understand you, I guess we've all had such feelings ... But I try as hard as I may to fight for happiness, and life of: *(...)* my Angels—they live as long as we have them in our hearts *(...)*. *[Jenny, F1]*

We can see here a reputation management process, which inevitably has to occur in a group initially anchored in the recognition of pain and suffering, which, although denied in the outside world, become one of the key group status markers. In doing so, the 'we' is reinstated ('we all have such feelings'), membership granted, and the boundaries of the group maintained. However, the maintenance of this group status marker is subtly renegotiated by also making clear what really 'matters'. The new constellation of feeling norms at stake here is one which grants superiority, in the hierarchy of feelings, to the reality of the 'life and happiness' of the unborn baby. This is done through the suppression of feelings of regret. This reveals that although access to the 'we' group is open for every individual who has suffered a perinatal loss, full status as an insider can only be accomplished through a realignment of the original feelings with the feeling norms of the community. The following exchange between another user of F1, 'Luna', and Jenny clearly illustrates this process:

> Luna: I'm reading all this stuff, and I see myself, my feelings … I'm very sorry that you have lost your little ones, it is so difficult to find any consolation… (…)
>
> Jenny: (…) and still I'm not able to say that I regret, because there was nothing more beautiful in my entire life than the time spent with my Kids (…).
>
> Luna: yes, these short moments with them [i.e. pregnancy before the loss] are the best that could have happened to us. At the beginning I didn't understand this and I repeated over and over again that I would have preferred not to have been pregnant than to suffer so much now, but I quickly understood that during this time I could feel that I was a mother and I could love with my whole heart. [F1]

Here, Luna clearly upholds and acknowledges the framing proposed by Jenny by offering a narrative of the transformation she has undergone since becoming a member of the community—she could not understand 'at the beginning', but exposure to the accounts and reactions of others quickly results in a rather radical change of feeling and redefinition of her own lived experience. In order to become insiders, these women must embrace a new conception of motherhood, redefined by supplanting any feelings of personal regret with the happiness of having been able to experience the unborn baby for whatever length of time this may have been. Acknowledging the reality of the unborn baby is crucial to their specific conception of motherhood which is being constructed here. We must recall that these women enter these particular online communities precisely because the outside world does not grant them the right to be treated as bona fide mothers, and this is done mostly through denying the status of babyhood of the unborn. Consequently, instituting the realness of the baby, through their redefinition of sadness as happiness for having had the opportunity to be mothers, however short the period of time, is key for them. They wish, above all, to legitimize their own lived experience of loss as an experience of genuine 'motherhood'. Regrets at being pregnant are perceived as a threat to this claim and therefore must be kept in check and redefined.

In line with the deference-emotion system as a constitutive method, this emerging conception of motherhood is constructed not only through the means of 'negative' forms of affective sanctioning (shaming and dishonoring mechanisms such as silencing, discrediting, and discouraging certain feelings), but also through the positive methods of conferring deference and honoring those certain views and feelings which are seen as fitting the emerging feeling norm. Honoring is exercised through actions such as displays of support and understanding. Like shaming, honoring, in the form of showing empathy for instance, also permeates interactions in these bereavement communities. When Jenny describes her story of miscarriage, she receives the following comments:

I can only say that I understand you perfectly well... (...) [Greta, F1]

I cried when I read what you wrote. This piece about growing up during one day ... After I lost [my son] I felt as if I got 10 years older... [Cindy, F1]

All the exchanges which reveal empathic responses ('I understand you all too well'/'I felt as if I was reading of myself'/'I cried when I read what you wrote') should be considered as instances of honoring which not only validate the individual's experience, but also constitute it as a shared collective good. Explicit positive descriptions of emotional reactions to what one user has written can be treated as the 'currency' in which honoring practices are expressed and a symbolic reward which is circulated and distributed (Barnes, 1995: 141). This is a particularly effective method to heighten personal feelings of worth and belonging, thus constraining deviance and fostering the necessary internal agreement and consensus for group forming and maintenance.

The 'we' as insiders is also developed by clearly delineating the outsiders, and this is also collectively achieved in and through the communication and exchange of personal accounts which incorporate a narrative of 'we' by expressing their feelings as widely shared. Fiona expresses this narrative of 'we' very clearly, in particular in how she reiterates one of the key claims circulating within these forums about the realness of the unborn. She describes how, despite having had children after the miscarriage of a previous pregnancy, regardless of what all the people around her told her, she is still feeling very poignantly the loss of the unborn baby:

> I am a worthless woman who is allergic towards the sight of women preg-
> nant and those with small kids … Maybe you'll say it's strange, because I
> have earth kids, but still, I also, much like you, feel worthless (…) because I
> lost my youngest Little One (…) I will always remember that there should
> be one more person [i.e. in her family]. [Fiona, F1]

Note the interesting categorical and classificatory distinction emerging
here between *earth* children and what has elsewhere been described by
many other mothers as 'Angel' children.[3] This distinction is aimed at giving the same (or at least similar in experiential and existential weight) status to the miscarried and the born babies. What Fiona proposes here is a
notable distinction from the dominant feeling norm of the outsiders who
attempt to console the bereaved women by insinuating that a new successful pregnancy and a living baby will make them forget their previous loss.
This, Fiona appears to suggest, has not only not happened to her but,
much to the contrary, the existence of the living earth babies have made
even stronger the longing for her lost baby. Her initial tentative 'maybe
you'll say it is strange' is pointing at the need for confirmation, a clear
indication that individually experienced feelings or emotions are never
fully recognized until they are confirmed by others. Fiona's account
receives an immediate and strong empathic response from other users, as
exemplified by Iga's response:

> I feel exactly the same. [Iga, F1]

Thus, a value hierarchy of feeling norms is established which is intrinsic of the 'we' group, and which clearly differentiates the insiders from
the outsiders. Not only accounts of feelings, but also new descriptive
categories emerge, which are directed to provide the expressive linguistic
vehicle suitable to convey, and account for, those subjective experiences
suppressed in the 'outside' world. Earth baby, Angel baby, and Angel's
mother slowly emerge as such new linguistic categories. By attributing
equal status to earth and Angel babies, these communities of women

---

[3] By choosing to use small letter for 'earth' baby and capitalize 'Angel' baby, we follow the
natural spelling used by the women whose entries we analyze. Throughout the discussions,
'earth' as an adjective used to denote born, living babies is never capitalized. In contrast,
'Angel' is sometimes capitalized when used as an adjective, and usually capitalized when used
as a noun and denoting 'lost unborn baby'.

redefine and reconceptualize the category of motherhood in a way which allows for the possibility and actualization of their emotional experiences of loss and grief.

The redefinition and reconceptualization of the categories of baby-hood and motherhood which these communities undertake clearly illustrate the open-ended nature of linguistic categories. This means that communities are always able to redefine existing categories, with new content and meaning, in order to adapt to new situations and experiences. Inter-subjective exchanges of an aggregate of mutually susceptible individuals engaging in interaction are a necessary precondition for such an operation of redefinition and reconstitution of new categories of experience. The constitution of new phenomena is a collective accomplishment, never an individual one. Once categories and practices are constituted as a collective good, they become reified as a reality in their own right. In the particular case of the women interacting in these bereavement forums, this social reality is in fact composed of the newly standardized feeling norms and value hierarchy, the adoption of which by its members constitutes the collective as a status group. The redefined experience of loss and grief becomes a collective good, the possession of which effects the distinction between the insiders and the outsiders, thus delineating group boundaries.

As we have noted throughout this section, the possibility of reclaiming the right to grief is founded on the redefinition of the realness of the unborn. In the next section, we turn our attention to the dynamics of how this redefinition takes place.

7.2.2   Establishing the Reality of the Unborn

The constitution of a new set of feeling norms and of a value hierarchy is a collective enterprise which involves generating a rationality internal to the group. As noted in the previous section, a considerable part of the discussion in these forums revolves around the theme of profound unhappiness experienced by these women, for not being allowed to count themselves as mothers in their communities of origin. Intimately related to this withdrawal of the motherhood status is the denial of their suffering. So, in order to be able to experience their grief as legitimate, these women will develop strategies to count themselves as bona fide mothers. The internally shared (in-group) rationality around their constructed sense of motherhood must, therefore, be rooted in the recognition and establishment of the reality of the lost babies. In this section we aim to trace different aspects of this process.

There are different ways in which the construction of the realness of the unborn baby takes place. One such way can be observed in the discussion about voluntary terminations of pregnancy. All mentions of abortion are extremely negatively sanctioned in these particular forums, to the point of seeking moderators to censor and exclude the presence of entries of such a nature. As one of the moderators noted:

> People after voluntary termination of pregnancy do not come to our forum, no-one. (...) Or they do not admit it, so a question arises if our forum is really a place for everyone? Probably not, because reactions towards people after termination are different [than towards people who involuntarily miscarried]. If somebody comes and is very repentant, which means she says she feels awful with what she has done, then the girls [other users] are able to show her some compassion. But if she comes and says (...) that she has terminated [the pregnancy] to be able to ... I will put it very straightforwardly, because she wanted to get rid of this problem to be able to get pregnant again, then the girls will not be willing to understand this so easily, they will be more prone to say 'hey, is there a moderator who can react?' and 'this is not a place for this person, our forum is not a place for such statements and such people'. [Interview no. 1]

That led her to conclude:

> This is not a place in the internet when one can say 'abortion'. This is noticeable. Here you can't—in the users' view—use the word 'abortion'. (...) This is taboo. [Interview no. 1]

This severely negative attitude towards abortion clearly aligns with the internal framing of the unborn baby as a full human being, worthy of risking a dangerous pregnancy, even in those cases of a fetus burdened with a lethal defect and where the mother's health may be at risk. This exclusionary practice further reinforces who is to be considered as a member of the 'we/insiders' and the 'other/outsiders'. The quotes above clearly reveal that there is a clash between two rationalities, and that only one of these is accepted within the group. The status of insiders is granted only to those individuals who align with the internal set of feeling norms. Membership of the 'we' group is constituted not only by the experience of losing a baby through perinatal loss or stillbirth, but also by the adoption of a collectively constituted framing of the situation of loss, and of the unborn itself. This framing, which is characterized by the love for an 'existing' baby since the moment of conception, is something that a voluntary abortion cannot be seen to abide by. A revealing instance, which further illustrates this mechanism, is the case of Kate, the protagonist of F2. Kate, against medical diagnosis and advice, decided to continue with the pregnancy despite the fetus being laden with a lethal defect. In her view, her unborn son 'had right to live as long as possible'. The robust honoring reaction of many members of the community towards her contrasts sharply with the negative sanctioning given to women who experienced voluntary terminations[4]:

You are such a strong person. Great strength is necessary to bear life which can disappear any moment... *[Alice, F2]*

and:

you are and you were a great mother for your son, having decided to continue the pregnancy you gave him a longer life, however still too short. Don't ever let anyone call you weak ... you've got great strength and love. *[Agnes, F2]*

Note that from the point of view of the outsiders—family members, doctors, friends—this framing is irrational: the rational course of action would have been to accept the medical diagnosis and advice, and to terminate this risky and doomed pregnancy. However, through a collective effort, the interacting collective reframes the course of action chosen by Kate as one of total rationality. This collectively constructed internal rationality is rooted in the key notion of reframing the unborn as having a life, and further establishing the reality of this life in the emerging category of an Angel baby. The Angel baby thus becomes a sacred object to the group. In this sense, the adoption of the terminology and attitudes that ensue towards the

---

[4] It is worth underlining that this seems not to be derivative of the religious views of the participants. Although according to public opinion polls the vast majority of Poles declare themselves as Catholics (since the 1990s the percentage has never been less than 90%, and currently stands at around 92%; for more see CBOS, 2018), the interviewees strongly stressed that the forum users are heterogeneous in this regard, being both Catholic and atheist. Moreover, the moderators note that often, remarks connected to religion and religious beliefs are silenced as inadequate, not pertaining to the 'core' of the issue (according to Interview nos. 1 and 2).

unborn and the doomed pregnancy becomes a key group status marker. In saying 'don't ever let anyone call you weak', they clearly signal that the opinion of outsiders doesn't count. Rather, what counts is the 'special honor' granted by insiders. In terms described earlier by Barnes and Collins, the attitude towards the unborn becomes a *constitutive symbol* of the new emerging ethnopsychology of shared feeling rules, and a key *organizer* of the communicative interaction of these groups. As one of the interviewees noted:

> probably there are people who would like to enter *[the forum]* and write straightforwardly 'I have never wanted to be pregnant, it is good that it turned out this way, and the only thing I want is to deal with the fact that I, as a person, as a woman, had to go through this ordeal', right? Like 'why it happened to me that I had to get pregnant although I had never wanted to and then I lost it', right? But it does not change the fact that *[this hypothetical user of the forum]* will not light candles now, because she doesn't want to go through this in this way. Because she is not grieving lost parenthood, but her own harmed self. And I think that this would be treated really negatively by the girls *[other users]*, really negatively. *[Interview no. 1]*

Thus, the sacrifice that Kate made for her unborn baby not only grants her the status of 'one of us', but also heightens her position in the internal group hierarchy as a woman who clearly places the unborn over and above her own personal health or suffering. This attitude is rationalized by the ontological grounding of the realness of the unborn, via the emphasis of being a parent (a mother in this case), even in the case of unborn babies:

> in Stockholm there are so many mothers with children :(Sometimes I wanted to cry out to them that I am also a mother but I can't walk with You *[the lost son]* because you're in Heaven :(*[Kate, F2]*

> Those were my children, they existed, and nothing will change it. *[Claire, F3]*

Establishing and redefining the reality of the unborn with new denoting categories such as Angel babies who live, but in heaven, allow for the cognitive attunement necessary for the emergence of a shared culture. References to the lost babies as Angels are pervasive in many exchanges:

> I wish you that the little one you carry under your heart will be healthy and give you a lot of happiness. It must be good *[=the pregnancy must finish well]* because there is an Angel who is taking care of the little one. *[F2, Kate]*

and:

[name], my little son, your mommy lighted a candle today and sang a lullaby for You and Your friend Angel [name], because, as you surely know, today it has been month since he was born. Play together and be good. *[F2, Kate]*

In many cases the users directly address the lost babies (their own or other users') by calling them 'Angels' and 'lighting' virtual candles, which is a common grieving practice in these communities:

Little Angel (∗∗∗) (∗∗∗) I hug your Mommy warmly. *[F2, Joyce]*
[name of the lost baby], Little Angel. *[F2, Rose]*
[name of the lost baby], little angel, for You (∗). *[F2, Claudia]*

The constitution of the lost baby as a *real* baby is pivotal to the redefinition of motherhood, which allows these women to contest and challenge the attitude to their grief received in their communities of origin. By denying the reality of the lost baby, they are denied the status of motherhood and therefore the right to mourn. A redefinition of the category of motherhood, different from that held in their communities of origin (which only grants motherhood status to women who have birthed living babies), is central to the accounts and exchanges in these forums, and in turn also to validating their right to experience and express their suffering.

7.2.3   Angels' Motherhood as a Collective Achievement

As we have observed, various types of affective sanctioning mechanisms are operationalized in order to achieve inter-subjective alignment and consensus among differing individuals. We have also seen how such an alignment generates a new set of shared feeling norms, underpinned by new descriptive and designating linguistic terms, which ontologically ground the reality of their experience. By establishing the reality of the unborn as an Angel baby with an ontologically equal status to the earth children, this community redefines motherhood in ways that better suit their personal (emotional) interests and needs—that is, it institutes an ontological foundation for their experience as mothers which allows for the expression of grief. According to this emerging reframing, women who have suffered a perinatal loss are now not only able, but also *entitled*, to think of themselves as mothers. Unlike their communities of origin, in these forums the designation of mother is an automatic status granted to all newcomers:

> Dear Mothers, I hug you warmly as well... *[Mary, F3]*

> Dear mum. It's true, there are so many of us here (and this is terrible). Write whatever you like, what you feel, what you think ... Each of us will help you, assist you. *[Bertha, F2]*

Because of the experience of being subjected to a set of exclusionary practices, a great part of the collective effort is invested in the redefinition and constitution of *a new conception of motherhood,* one which can enable the bereaved women to harmonize their feelings (pain and suffering after the loss) with their actual situation (the lack of physical traces of the baby, i.e. pictures or clothes, as well as a wider recognition of the 'baby' status prenatally). On a par with the categorization of the lost baby as an Angel baby, the reconceptualization of motherhood takes the designation of an Angel's mother, and is significant in observing the immediate constitutive effect it has upon newcomers:

> Greetings to all Angels' Mothers. *(...)* I like this name very much and thank you for using it because thanks to it for the first time I thought of myself as of a mother. *[Mary, F3]*

> Honestly, before I found this site and this forum, I hadn't thought of myself as of a 'mom'. *[Luna, F1]*

The silencing and suppressing practices of the communities of origin are revealed here in all their efficacious nature, insofar as they appear to foreclose any possibility of 'thinking' of themselves as mothers at all. However, this is also very significant, as it reveals how open-ended and fluid these subjective feelings are, as these women need very little 'training' to rethink of themselves as mothers—a clear illustration of the continuous created nature of social life, and individual subjectivity. It is also poignant to observe how the reference to the use of the category appears to effect such a change—a demonstration of the performative force of linguistic speech acts. Having established the reality of the non-living baby through the signifying category of Angel babies, the possibility of motherhood is now also established as a real experience for these women. Claims about the reality of the experience of motherhood are voiced in two distinct ways during the interactive exchanges on the forums. Sometimes they take the explicit form of users' declarations addressed to other interactants:

> I also cannot forget my little son ... I don't want to forget ... He was in my heart from the very beginning and he will be there always ... I felt I was a mother from the very beginning (...) [Mary, F3]

> We will surely never forget what happened, Our Children will always be in our hearts (...) remember, you're a Mother! [Grace, F3]

> I believe that a child is a child from the very beginning and we have right to feel we are mothers who lost their little ones. No matter how many weeks they had. [Greta, F1]

Other times, they are articulated indirectly through emphasis placed on the intensity of feelings of maternal love towards the Angel baby:

> You love your baby from the very beginning, you are connected to it with such a strong bond that it cannot be described :(I was always moved by the words placed on the vitamins for pregnant women which I took: I don't know You yet, but I already love You! [Grace, F3]

> she will always be my first child for me—my daughter [name of the lost baby]. I fell in love with her so much when for the first time I saw on the screen [of the ultrasound] her little head, hands, legs. [Joyce, F3]

And in the exchange between Kate and Caroline on F2, Kate describes that when she shared with her family the information that the fetus she was carrying had a lethal defect, some of the family members started to avoid visiting her, in an attempt—as Kate supposes—to avoid the emotional suffering which would be brought about by the imminent loss.

> Kate: One of my closest relatives told me recently that when [Kate's son] was alive [i.e. Kate was pregnant] she didn't come around too often, because she didn't want to get emotionally engaged. This is only human ... We had to devote ourselves fully to our little ones, but it doesn't mean that everyone had to suffer that much...

> Caroline: You're right, we gave ourselves fully to our little ones, because we love them with all our strength, and not everyone is capable of this [such love]. [F2]

Angels' mothers are accorded equal status to that granted to earth mothers, insofar as the intensity of the feeling of love is made equivalent to that of an earth mother. Thus, through a collective effort, a new ethno-psychology of motherhood emerges which entitles the community members to mourn after their losses and recognizes their sorrow as justified and vindicated.

This newly acquired motherhood status grants recognition, but only if the members of the community abide by the internal feeling norms instituted. The new ethnopsychology grants certain rights to the insiders, but also burdens them with inherent obligations. The accounts exchanged within the communities about these obligations reveal the construction of further layers of meaning attributed to their adopted category of motherhood. Angels' mothers are framed as *custodians* of their Angel babies' memory, and as such their paramount obligation is to be faithful to their 'Angels' no matter what. Such faithfulness often demands extreme actions, such as the rejection of a dominant external rationality which advises against continuing endangered pregnancies for medical reasons. This is not to say that these women reject any possibility of future attempts to achieve successful pregnancies, but rather that they commit themselves to mourning the lost baby for as long as possible, even if this means postponing potential future pregnancies.

Accordingly, the rule of devotion to the memory of the lost Angels become an obligatory emotional norm in these communities, because the women have redefined the ontological status of the unborn as real and, consequently, also their experience of motherhood as true and real. In the same way that society could not expect a mother to lose the memory of an 'earth' child in the event of death, within these communities Angels' mothers are granted the same right and expected to act accordingly. This is especially visible in all accounts in which they make comparisons between Angel and earth babies, or when describing the experience of being mothers to both Angel and earth babies:

> *[Kate]*, your son will always be in your memory. I know from my own experience, when I walk with *[the name of Rose's existing son]* I think all the time how it would be to walk with *[the name of Rose's lost daughter]*, I see her everywhere :(nothing will ever take her place for me :(*[Rose, F2]*

Further, Rose underlines:

> I love *[the son]* very much, but I have *[the lost daughter]* in my heart all the time and will always keep her there, until I die. *[Rose, F2]*

In Alice's account, the painful intensity of the memory of the lost baby has even been increased, rather than diminished, by the very fact of getting pregnant again:

I can't deny that *[since getting pregnant again]* my appetite has grown a lot … but I do not cook, *[the husband]* is angry on me because of that, that I don't give a damn for anything … but I keep telling him that now I should cook dinners for our little son, but he is not here, and so the dinners won't be here as well… *[Alice, F2]*

This makes visible the newly constructed rationality, in which it does not make sense to make the effort to cease or minimize their grieving, as is expected of them in their communities of origin. As a community, they have constructed their internal feeling rules and values with an alternative rationality—one which allows them to fully express and feel their suffering. Being 'faithful to one's Angels', by honoring their memory, constitutes the self and identity as an Angel's mother, and institutes obligations in line with this new rationality of what is expected from them towards the unborn, the pregnancy, and motherhood. These obligations entail love for the unborn since the moment of conception; lack of regret over the doomed pregnancy despite physical and psychological suffering; granting a higher status to the unborn 'self' over and above the mother's; a willingness to admit and defend a firm ontological status of the realness of the unborn baby, in equal terms to live children; and to being a faithful guardian of their memory.

These obligations will become essential signifiers of group status markers within these communities of bereaved women, of what is to be taken to be, and experienced as, motherhood. Not all individuals whose pregnancies are terminated prematurely are automatically considered insiders by the Angels' mothers communities. Accepting and partaking in the internally held ethnopsychology of feeling rules is essential to acquire the status of 'membership'. The status of membership, and the new identity which it grants, are only available to those individuals who are willing to modify, and reframe, their feelings and practices to those held by the community. Angel motherhood membership comes with rights (legitimation and validation of the personal feelings of suffering, which are suppressed in their communities of origin) and obligations towards other members of the community and to themselves, to adopt the feeling rules of the internal ethnopsychology of motherhood. Collectively sharing and participating in this understanding of motherhood constitute Angel motherhood as a social institution intrinsic to the group. As such, it acquires the status of macro-phenomena; that is, while emerging from the group it becomes reified, gaining the practical objectivity necessary for the group to function as a life-world. As a result, it circumscribes and exercises a causal force on the practices, beliefs, and feelings of the members belonging to, or wishing to belong to, these communities.

7.3   ETHNOPSYCHOLOGIES AND THEIR INTERSECTIONS

In what has been developed in this chapter, we have focused on illuminating the processes and mechanisms by which a new ethnopsychology emerges, or, to be more precise, how a new set of shared beliefs about emotions is constituted in and through the micro-dynamics of group interaction. We have followed in some detail how a subjective emotional experience, denied the crucial status of 'being real' in an (out-group) ethnopsychology, becomes ontologically grounded in another (in-group) ethnopsychology. We have shown how this is achieved through a collective effort aimed at redefining the linguistic categories through which these individuals regain a sense of belonging which will underpin validation and legitimation of their subjective experience of loss and grief. We have argued that in and through this collective effort of validation, a new ontological grounding is effected based on the redefinitions of the content and meaning of babyhood and motherhood, generating the necessary sense of realness in which to ground them.

With this, we aimed to illustrate the superior analytical merits of an intrinsic structuralist account which envisages social life as in a continuous creation mode and open-ended in nature. We have operationalized this model to shed light on how certain ethnopsychologies of motherhood, such as that of Angels' mothers, materialize within particular collectives in and through the constitution of internal group status markers, which, while anchored in categories existing in the actors' community of origin, are redefined within the collectives in order to fulfill their particular interests and needs. We have shown how group status markers such as Angel motherhood and Angel babyhood are rooted in aspects such as the legitimacy of the suffering of the mother, the happiness of the unborn baby, the elevated status of the unborn baby over the mother, its equal or higher status over living (or potential) siblings, and—above all—the reality of its existence.

Such an approach fosters a critical understanding of the interconnections between existing ethnopsychologies and the wider cultural narratives within which they are immersed. Understanding social reality as open-ended allows for an explanation of the emergence of social phenomena within localized collectives, but also, significantly, sheds light on the co-constitutive dynamics between subcultures of a society and the general narratives of the society at large. Unlike those extrinsic structuralist models which adopt a reproductive orientation, the intrinsic structuralist model we develop here sees social change as not only possible, but inevitable.

Ethnopsychologies treated as intrinsic structural phenomena should be seen as characterized by two crucial features. Firstly, each ethnopsychology should be regarded as a 'constant construction site'. Ethnopsychologies, like any other social phenomena, are constantly created and recreated by individuals interacting with each other and in the process generating new meanings, rules, and practices. Secondly, such 'construction sites' should be seen as separated from the outside world by a semi-permeable 'membrane', as it were, much like the one which encloses the inside of a living cell. Individual members of the groups cross this 'membrane' in and out quite often as they belong to several groups simultaneously. In doing so, they bring in and out cultural categories existing within the groups as they 'travel' back and forth. In this way, they expose the meaning and content of the categories they use in their different collectives to a constant feedback loop. This idea is visually presented in Fig. 7.1.

No social life, and no social phenomenon, ever emerges from a blank canvas. All categories and practices are derived from categories, meanings, and practices which already exist and are available to individuals who enter into new collectives. Existing categories operate as background knowledge, offering a base which creative human collectives can elaborate, and in which new, reformulated categories and meanings will be grounded. As the content and meaning of existing categories are open-ended—that is, never fully fixed and determined—when categories are used in other contexts with different personal and cultural requirements, individuals are able to redefine them to suit their needs. In the case of the online bereavement communities discussed here, what are used as 'bricks' for the construction of new linguistic categories are some of the elements of the already existing cultural imaginary—products of previously constituted ethnopsychologies—which are brought *into* the new ethnopsychology and redefined to construct the concept of Angel motherhood. Knowledge of both past and present Polish discourses of motherhood enables us to

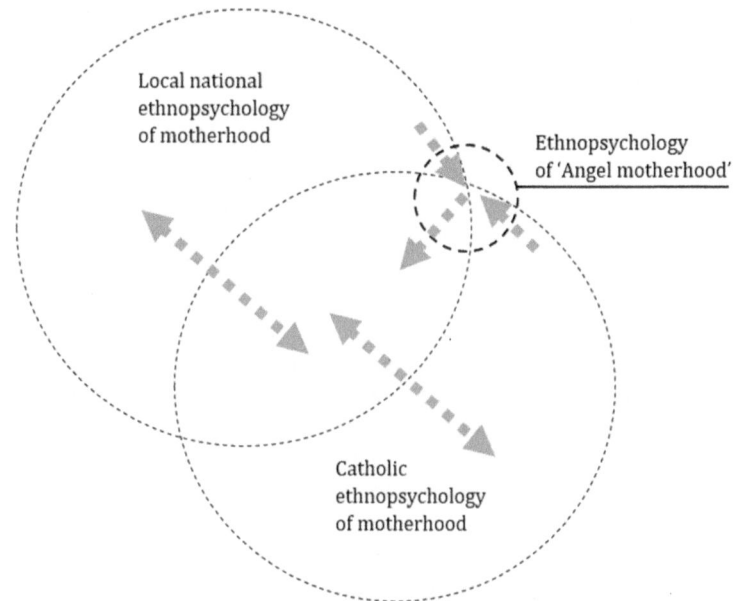

Fig. 7.1   Angel motherhood ethnopsychology and its intersections

identify the 'bricks' which serve as the building blocks for the ethnopsychology of Angel motherhood. We can identify two such fundamental
building blocks of this particular ethnopsychology.

Firstly, the sanctity of the life of an unborn baby is strongly advocated
by the Catholic Church. Since 1993, the year in which a new abortion act
was introduced in Poland,[5] there has been a continuing dispute in Polish
society between fractions opposing the act, advocating for more liberal
access to legal abortion, and those who support further restrictions,
including fully delegalizing abortion. Social actors who lobby against a

---

[5] Current regulations on the access to legal abortion in Poland are already more restrictive
than in most European countries and allow abortion only in three cases: when the life of the
pregnant woman is endangered due to pregnancy, when the pregnancy results from a crimi-
nal act, and when based on medical investigation it can be inferred that the fetus is burdened
with a serious defect (Ustawa o planowaniu rodziny, ochronie płodu ludzkiego i warunkach
dopuszczalności przerywania ciąży z dn. 7 stycznia 1993 [Polish bill on family planning,
protection of human fetus, and conditions for termination of pregnancy introduced on
January 7, 1993]).

right to legal abortion are connected to the Catholic Church in Poland. These fractions use religious categories to talk about the beginnings of human life and, importantly, substitute medical and rather technical terms like 'fetus' or 'embryo' with the more emotionally loaded term 'unborn baby'.

The term 'unborn baby' is a key linguistic category used by members of Catholic 'pro-life' movements, and connects two essential notions fundamental for the Polish Catholic ethnopsychology of motherhood. The first of these notions is a particular conception of human life: that the fetus or embryo is conceived as a 'human being', since human life is thought to begin at the very moment of conception. The second notion is that this 'being', at this perinatal stage, is of the most fragile and dependent kind, and as such it deserves extra special care, such as legal protection in form of anti-abortion regulations. Religiously motivated collectives of 'pro-life' movements apply the category of 'unborn baby' especially to pregnancies that can be terminated because of medical necessity or legal possibility (for instance, calling for prayers or the 'spiritual adoption' of 'unborn babies endangered with abortion'). The religious discourse, and the Catholic ethnopsychology of motherhood, in which the terms 'fetus' and 'embryo' are substituted by the term 'unborn baby', provide Angels' mothers with this key linguistic category to be applied to pregnancies. In this sense, the category 'Angel baby' coined within Angels' mothers collectives is anchored in an existing conceptualization of a baby yet unborn, but already existing, and then it is internally redefined in terms which suit the particular needs and interests of the women on these forums.

Another core constituent of Angel's motherhood which we have identified is the belief that motherhood is defined by suffering. This equating of motherhood with suffering is also anchored in broader existing framings of motherhood in Polish society, and can be traced back to the wider cultural archetype of a 'Polish Mother', which emerged through a turbulent period of Polish history. In the nineteenth century, Poland was occupied by its neighbors, Prussia, Austria, and Russia (this period is commonly referred to as the 'partitions' of Poland), and had no legal identity. During the partitions period, all political activity aimed at regaining national independence was banned. Safeguarding Polish national consciousness relied on the general population: men participated in consecutive armed uprisings against the invaders, while women were expected to take a different burden. First of all, they were to safeguard the memories of Poland as a free country and pass them to the next generations, so that the idea of a free Polish nation could thrive in the hearts of Polish people. Secondly, they were to 'sacrifice their sons' to the national cause, educating their children in the patriotic spirit and allowing, or even encouraging, them to join the armed resistance efforts. Hence comes the archetype of *Mater dolorosa*, who sacrifices her son for the cause (Bernini, 2015). As well as the political and ideological content, there is also a religious link in this archetype of motherhood. The Polish Mother, in her suffering, bears a resemblance to Mary, the mother of Jesus Christ who sacrificed his life to save humanity. The cult of the Holy Mary is deeply rooted in Polish religiosity and culture, in which she is often depicted as a mother full of sorrow, grieving her lost son. However, her grief and sorrow should not be mistaken for weakness; rather, by embracing and partaking in her son's suffering, she acquires a powerful and elevated queen-like status which denotes strength (Trochimczyk, 2003).

We may infer that both these archetypes, 'Polish Mother' and 'Holy Mother', provide Angels' mothers with three key features in which they can anchor their unique ethnopsychology of motherhood: that motherhood is constituted by the suffering of a mother who mourns her lost offspring; that what constitutes a mother is that she is the custodian of the past, responsible for safeguarding precious collective memories, a component of the Polish Mother archetype; and that the lost offspring are powerful beings with special abilities, real Angels able to take care of the earth family, make their mother conceive again, and look after their earth siblings, an idea which is the core of the Holy Mother archetype. We can identify traces of this archetype of motherhood existing in the narratives of the wider Polish society in the ethnopsychology of Angel motherhood, for which key group status markers are the acclamation of the suffering of the mother, an obligation to preserve the memory of the lost baby and be 'faithful' to the Angel baby, and a belief that the lost baby is an Angel, that is, a good and protective spirit.

We can see how the concept of Angel motherhood, constructed by the members of these communities, does not emerge in isolation from the existing wider cultural narratives and practices of the society in which they operate. Rather, it uses and reconstructs existing categories as foundational building blocks. As we have noted, however, the feedback loop goes both ways. Newly constructed meanings and categories travel back and forth between collectives, mutually influencing each other's internally held ethnopsychologies and thus generating cultural transformation. The notion of Angel baby, adopted by the Angels' mothers groups, although still residing at the margins of the dominant emotional culture in Poland, has already exercised some influence on it. For instance, due to the efforts of an organization for parents after perinatal loss (to which one of the forums analyzed belongs), in 2004 a special Remembrance Day was introduced in Poland, called 'the Lost Child's Day', to be celebrated on 15 October. Although this Remembrance Day was inspired by the American 'Pregnancy and Infant Loss Remembrance Day', proclaimed in 1988,[6] its adoption in Poland almost two decades later clearly indicates that Polish society had become sensitive to the new categorizations emerging from the Angels' mothers ethnopsychology operating at the time in the forums analyzed.

Another example of the influence of the Angel motherhood ethnopsychology can perhaps be found in a 2018 bill regulating guidelines for healthcare professionals in Poland. In the bill, the description of miscarriage/stillbirth was reworded, substituting 'midwifery failure' with 'special circumstances'. This very deliberate change in wording, approved on January 1, 2019,[7] clearly aligns with how the Angels' mothers groups frame their lost pregnancies. As demonstrated in the empirical sections of this book, Angels' mothers do not frame lost pregnancies as a 'failure'. On the contrary, this framing is applied by the outsiders, whose view they fully reject. In the Angel motherhood ethnopsychology, having been pregnant for even a short period of time is treated as a privilege and safeguarded as a precious memory. The term 'midwifery failure' is rooted in a rationality in which the aim is to give birth to a living and healthy baby. Its replacement by a more delicate phrase, 'special circumstances', can be seen as a sign of growing sensitivity for the feelings of women who have miscarried, and the meanings which they attach to their loss.

Both these events should be regarded as symptoms of cultural change, initiated by the inter-relation between groups' internally constituted macro-phenomena. New redefinitions emerging from one group can influence and trigger a process of redefinition from another, thus instigating wider cultural changes. More explanatory and specific detail on how this migration, transfer, and mutual influence of inter-related collectives operate would require further empirical investigation. For instance, it

[6] According to Polish Wikipedia, notes on the entry 'Dzień Dziecka Utraconego' ('the Lost Child's Day').
[7] Source: https://legislacja.rcl.gov.pl/docs//516/12310054/12499721/12499722/dokument335859.pdf [retrieved 09.07.2018, 10:00].

would require identifying aspects such as: Which actors are involved in the process? What are the specific political and ideological conditions in which these changes take place? Which groups do such changes benefit? What kind of accounts and rationale are given to justify the changes? Such an empirical investigation would offer not only an analytically intriguing path for future research, but also a very useful insight into the mutually co-constitutive dynamics between different groups' subcultures existing in a particular society. And in doing so, it would further illuminate the social foundations of the nature of social reality.

BIBLIOGRAPHY

Barnes, B. (1995). *The Elements of Social Theory*. London, UK: UCL Press.

Bernini, S. (2015). Mothers and Children in Post-War Europe: Martyrdom and National Reconstruction in Italy and Poland. *European Review of History: Revue européenne d'histoire, 22*(2), 242–258.

CBOS. (2018). *Religijność Polaków i ocena sytuacji Kościoła Katolickiego*. Survey Report No. 147/2018.

Hazen, M. A. (2003). Societal and Workplace Responses to Perinatal Loss: Disenfranchised Grief or Healing Connection. *Human Relations, 56*(2), 147–166.

James, W. R. (2000). Placing the Unborn: On the Social Recognition of New Life. *Anthropology & Medicine, 7*(2), 169–189.

Keefe-Cooperman, K. (2004 [2005]). A Comparison of Grief as Related to Miscarriage and Termination for Fetal Abnormality. *OMEGA, 50*(4), 281–300.

Lang, A., Fleiszer, A. R., Duhamel, F., Sword, W., Gilbert, K. R., & Corsini-Munt, S. (2011). Perinatal Loss and Parental Grief: The Challenge of Ambiguity and Disenfranchised Grief. *OMEGA, 63*(2), 183–196.

Sawicka, M. (2017). Searching for a Narrative of Loss: Interactional Ordering of Ambiguous Grief. *Symbolic Interaction, 40*(2), 229–246.

Thoits, P. A. (1990). Emotional Deviance. In T. Kemper (Ed.), *Research Agenda for Sociology of Emotions* (pp. 180–203). New York, NY: SUNY.

Trochimczyk, M. (2003). Mater Dolorosa and Maternal Love in Górecki's Music. *Polish Music Journal* (6)2, Online Publication. Retrieved March 20, 2019, from https://polishmusic.usc.edu/research/publications/polish-music-journal/vol6no2/mater-dolorosa-and-maternal-love-in-goreckis-music/

CHAPTER 8

Concluding Points: Theoretical Models, Social Reality, and Everyday Practice

Abstract The concluding chapter summarizes the key points, both of the theoretical model and of the empirical investigation into online bereavement communities. It concludes that there is an implicit individualistic bias in most emotion theory and research. The authors' theoretical development demonstrates that any cultural frame that is placed on individual feelings in fact emerges from the micro-dynamics of interaction, and, thus, should be considered a collective achievement. A position which acknowledges the collective and processual dimension of individuals' emotional experiences implies a particular understanding of agency: instead of focusing on isolated individuals and their pre-established dispositions imprinted through primary socialization, it calls for taking into consideration the continuous constitutive role happening *between* people when they interact with others, in particular the role of emotional pressures (in terms of affective sanctioning) and the bonds that emerge from social interactions between members of a status group. Practical implications of this claim are presented, including those relevant for moderators of digital support groups, healthcare professionals dealing with parents after perinatal loss, and, more generally, policy practice. It is argued that effective intervention must consider the collective nature of social life and recognize that individual practices are intrinsically grounded in group dynamics.

Keywords Agency • Digital support groups • Online moderators • Healthcare • Perinatal loss • Policy practice

© The Author(s) 2020   99
I. Rafanell, M. Sawicka, *Emotions in Digital Interactions*,
https://doi.org/10.1007/978-3-030-21998-7_8

In this book, we aimed to provide a conceptual apparatus which we believe enhances both an analytical and empirical understanding of social life, its emerging patterns, and ordering practices. We offered a conception of social life in which the social world is seen as created and maintained by the continuous activity of individuals in a situated space of action. This turned our analytical focus to the ways (the methods used by such individuals) through which this interactive activity is performed, and to the collectivist, rather than individualistic, nature of social life. In this sense, the implications of this research are both analytical and methodological, insofar as the relationship between the subjective perspective and the objective world has taken on a particular social constructionist orientation. Analytically, we aimed to demonstrate the merits of an intrinsic structuralist model for the understanding of how individual subjective experience is intimately connected with the construction of the social phenomena which circumscribes it, and emphasized the co-constitutive relationship between the subjective and the social. Methodologically, we built upon the phenomenological and ethnomethodological prescription that in order to understand the emergence of social life, attention must be placed on the methods used in the inter-subjective dynamics which underpin the generation of consensus and agreement.

We revealed how social reality is constructed in and through the exchanges taking place among a set of mutually susceptible individuals, and identified different elements which are implicated in this process. We noted that inherent to any linguistic acts is a process of reification a process of the making of 'things-like'—that is, when those 'things' being referred to acquire qualities of objectivity and externality. In our investigation, we highlighted this process of reality creation taking place in online forums of bereaved women, who had suffered miscarriage or perinatal loss. We highlighted how the exclusionary practices experienced in their communities of origin, through which members of these communities negate the emotional expression of loss, is the basis of generating support groups which allow for the manifestation and exchange of their suffering. We investigated how their individual accounts were exposed to the inter-subjective dynamics of evaluative practices, which in turn constituted the internally held ethnopsychology of feeling norms. We identified the methods used by the members of these collectives to inter-evaluate each other's accounts and how, from this process, new terminology emerges which ontologically grounds their personal experience of loss and grief. We argued that emerging terminology, such as Angel babies and Angels' mothers, effects a reification of the feeling norms as a shared property, thus becoming the macro-phenomena which in turn circumscribe individual practices. These linguistic terms, we argued, redefine existing categorizations of babyhood and motherhood from their communities of origin, allowing the members of these groups to constitute a new object of reference as an external reality intrinsic to these groups. We have noted that these new categorizations underpin group formation by virtue of becoming key status group markers of group membership.

Utilizing Barnes' emphasis on the constitutive force of acts of reference, we further emphasized the process of reification taking place when a localized group of interactants engages in linguistic acts of reference. In doing so, we highlighted the local, contextual, contingent, and open-ended nature of social life. One key analytical point we aimed to demonstrate is that arguing that social life must be seen as a continuous accomplishment emerging from the micro-dynamics of interaction within a group of individuals does not ignore social reality or macro-structural phenomena. On the contrary, we argued that the analytical model we have developed provides a clear referent to an external social reality. However, it understands social reality differently than other theoretical accounts. Rather than conceiving social reality as external and independent from individuals' interactions and yet determining them, we argued that social reality should be perceived as emerging from the performative force of collective acts of reference, exchanged by inter-connected and mutually susceptible individuals. We described social reality as self-referential, in the sense that the object of reference is constituted in and through the collective of acts of reference of such inter-connected individuals, and therefore is intrinsic to group dynamics, rather than extrinsic. As an empirical demonstration of such an analytical framework, we investigated the processes and methods through which specific groups of individuals in given online bereavement communities accomplish this process of the reification of social reality, and how it helps them to ontologically ground their subjective experience.

By adopting the ethnomethodological focus on the methods individuals operationalize in interactions with one another, rather than the discovery of any presupposed existing reality, we aimed to identify, isolate, and uncover specific types of methods employed by the members of online communities to accomplish this 'reality construction'. We applied Scheff's analytical framework of a deference-emotion system to identify specific sanctioning practices for individuals' actions which use honoring and dishonoring evaluative accounts in the form of priding and shaming. We argued that these evaluative accounts are predominant methods used by individuals, interacting with one another in localized social settings, to achieve realignment and agreement with one another, thus constituting collectively held normative standards of a new ethnopsychology of motherhood.

In tune with the ethnomethodological and social constructionist framework we develop in this book, the methodological orientation we implement is one which aims to uncover how social phenomena *come to exist*, rather than to address any presupposed existing social reality. This interest is rooted in the philosophical underpinnings of constructionist positions vis-à-vis the nature of social reality. We argued that sociological theories which neglect to pay attention to how social reality emerges and adopt an understanding of social reality as an objective given of discoverable structures (Thomason, 1982) fail to provide convincing explanations of either the nature of the *reality* of the social or individual agency.

In Part I, we presented the analytical framework developed to guide our empirical investigation. This framework emerged from an amalgamation of different social constructionist approaches, such as ethnomethodology, symbolic interactionism, and aspects of the sociology of knowledge of Barnes and Bloor. We started by presenting a discussion of differing positions on what counts as social reality. We identified two broad positions emerging from adopting, unwittingly or explicitly, a different ontological understanding of what counts as social reality. There are those theoretical positions which assume a more positivist orientation, understanding social reality as existing objectively 'out there' (noumena), independent of individuals' perceptions of it—and yet exercising a determining force on individuals' practices. On the other hand, we expanded on those positions which adopt a more constructionist approach and understand social reality as emerging from individuals' representations, or accounts, of it (phenomena).

We moved on to argue that the former suffer from a lack of analytical depth, rendering them unable to explain convincingly the emergence and nature of social reality, nor the mechanics of how it determines individual action. We developed this critique by presenting Bourdieu's theoretical model as paradigmatic of a theoretical model unwittingly adopting a positivistic approach by refusing, in particular, to acknowledge the role of the micro-dynamics of interaction in the construction of structural social reality. We argued that this results in adopting a theoretical model which conceives social reality as constructed at one point (though leaving unexplained what this point of origin is) and subsisting, from then on, independently of individuals' actions, acquiring a permanent determining force. In other words, these models effect a process of reification of social reality which renders it ontologically separate from individual action, conceptualizing reality as an objective given. We name these positions *extrinsic structuralist* accounts of social reality, which convey an overdeterministic stance and deny the constitutive role of individuals' agency and practice. This results in a particular conception of social reality which perceives the macro-structural world as external to, and operating from the outside upon, individuals' actions. We argued that sociologists of emotions, such as Gordon, tacitly adopt this theoretical orientation by explaining emotions as fully caused by macro-structural arrangements, thus neglecting to acknowledge any causal role emotions may have in the emergence of structural reality. We aimed to demonstrate how these theoretical positions neglect how individuals operate in the world, and disregard the mechanisms involved in negotiating inter-action and inter-subjectivities, because they see individuals as products of macro-structural determinants which shape and mold their actions.

In contrast to such overdeterministic accounts, we presented an analytical framework amalgamating analytical insights from ethnomethodologists, symbolic interactionists, and sociologists of knowledge, to develop a constructionist account which allows for a more analytically rigorous understanding of the interplay between structural phenomena and individual practice. We described these positions as *intrinsic structuralism*, insofar as they strive to explain social reality as emerging from, and continuously created and maintained by, a community of mutually susceptible interacting individuals. We noted that such a perspective adopts a continuous creation model: a theoretical model which conceives macro-structural phenomena as internal, inseparable, and originating from individuals' interactive activity, and one which understands micro-situational dynamics as the 'ground zero' of all social phenomena and social action (Collins, 2005). We highlighted that these positions share a methodological orientation signified by their emphasis on the constitutive force of the *methods* employed by individuals engaged in making sense of one another's accounts when engaged in interactive dynamics. The methodological orientation which these constructionist positions espouse is that these methods must be identified, rather than presupposed, by a careful elucidation of what happens when individuals engage in sharing their subjective experiences and accounts of the world they live in.

In order to further develop such an intrinsic structuralist analytical model, we presented the work of the sociologists of knowledge Barnes and Bloor. From Barnes, we adopted his performative theory of social institutions and his conceptualization of social life as self-referential in nature—individual acts of reference constitute the object which is being referred to. We noted how Barnes distinguishes between acts of reference to natural kinds of reality (which are, to an extent, informed by an existing external object) and acts of reference to social kinds of reality (which are informed by *how*, and *what*, other members of the community refer to as such). Barnes, thus, makes individual acts of reference dependent on the whole of the collective, and conceives the emergence of social reality as the accomplishment of an interactive collective of mutually susceptible (not singular and isolated) individuals. From Bloor, we harnessed his theory of meaning finitism, which conceives the meaning and content of the categories used to describe reality as open-ended and underdetermined. Bloor's contention is that in order to achieve consensus and meaning stability (and practice), individuals operationalize an internal set of normative standards via constant examination with one another of their individual accounts. Both Barnes and Bloor argue that collective agreement on meaning and action emerges from internal evaluative sanctioning practices, which grant correctness and incorrectness to individual accounts vis-à-vis the internally held set of knowledge and normative standards.

Following this, we noted that contrary to the extrinsic models, which conceive individuals as internalizing norms, beliefs, and practices once and for all, the intrinsic model we presented understands that individuals are heterogeneous, and that, even though they are exposed to existing structural determinants, they are never fully socialized. Rather than being conceived as having an agency determined through permanent dispositional inclinations, individual practice should be conceived as provisional and open-ended. Individuals' subjective experience and individual accounts must be confirmed and corroborated by others in order to generate a collective consensus and for individuals themselves to make sense of them. In other words, they must be internally sanctioned. We complemented Barnes' and Bloor's emphasis on the need for internal collective sanctioning—to generate consensus and meaning stability, and therefore social reality—by using Scheff's theorization of what he calls the deference-emotion system. Scheff draws attention to the constitutive role of particular affective sanctioning mechanisms, in the form of honoring and dishonoring, which are ubiquitously used in interaction to ensure alignment and minimize deviation by individuals from the collectively held normative standards. Using the work of Scheff, we noted that such inter-evaluative sanctioning practices operationalize, in particular, the emotions of pride and shame. Scheff notes that individuals are susceptible to signs of approval and disapproval from other individuals in their immediate social environment. Consequently, individuals tend to avoid being discredited by others and, especially, avoid feelings of shame—as these are profoundly connected with their subjective sense of self-esteem and self-worth. Such affective sanctioning mechanisms result in the restraining of deviance, generate inter-individual alignment, and ensure the flow of inter-group interaction. It is in this sense that priding and shaming practices should be conceived as key methods underpinning the constitution of social phenomena.

We highlighted that the constitutive role of affective sanctioning methods is twofold: emotions are both operationalized to monitor others, and internalized as self-monitoring practices. In and through this process, both the external objects of reference (social reality) and personal subjective experience are redefined and reconstituted. Overall, we stressed that social life must be conceived as local, situated, and contextual. In other words, individuals' actions and interactions must be located within collectives which operate as status groups. As such, individuals strive to avoid negative evaluations from members of those collectives they wish to belong to, and in doing so they abide by, and further constitute, the internally held group status markers. Such status group markers are constitutive of the group boundary, as a community whose members share a common language and which forms a distinctive subculture; they signal what is to be considered as the insider and the outsider, and the normative standards to be held; and they construct an internal rationality which guides practice and ensures internal consensus and agreement. From this, reconceptualized forms of social reality emerge, which are considered collective goods to be protected, and which define group membership and ensure smooth communicative interaction.

Based on the overall methodological premise of the analytical framework developed in Part I, Part II presented an empirical investigation of three online communities of bereaved parents who have experienced perinatal loss. We focused on examining and analyzing different elements involved in the constitutive dynamics of communicative interaction, group formation, and internally held normative standards. Our attention was directed, specifically, to identifying the affective sanctioning methods operationalized by members of the group, in and through communicative exchanges, and the emergence of redefined social categories signifying new social phenomena.

We began by exploring the underlying motivations which encourage these individuals to join online bereavement forums. A key feature which emerged from this exploration was a commonly experienced feeling of exclusion from their communities of origin, by virtue of the suppression, or denial, of the articulation and expression of the suffering they experience in relation to loss and grief. By analyzing the accounts provided and exchanged by the members of these online forums, we identified that such a denial was experienced as deriving from the existing ethnopsychology of motherhood of their communities of origin—one which only grants the status of babyhood to offspring born alive. As a consequence of such a belief, the status of motherhood is felt to be granted only to women who have birthed live babies, thus effectively withdrawing such a status from women who have experienced perinatal loss—and with it, the right to communicate, and experience, their subjective feelings of motherly loss and grief. Negative evaluative statements towards their expression of suffering, dishonoring of their feelings by depicting them as inappropriate or prejudicial to their peers' wellbeing, and shaming displays of emotional grief and lack of empathy and sympathy, all emerged as methods utilized within these communities to attempt to realign the perceived deviant women, back in line with the normative standards intrinsic to their ethnopsychology of motherhood.

Motivated by the experience of exclusion and lack of social recognition within their communities of origin, these women seek support in alternate social arenas. They find this support in online support forums for bereaved parents who have suffered perinatal loss. When entering the online forums, these women already share a similar experience of resistance to exclusionary practices and lack of recognition and, therefore, are granted the status of belonging. Our exploration of the communicative interactions and exchanges within these online forums revealed the emergence of redefined conceptions of babyhood and motherhood, which underpinned the emergence of a new ethnopsychology of motherhood. Categories such as Angel baby and Angel's mother emerge to fulfill specific aims, needs, and interests of the women belonging to such forums; to wit, the validation and legitimation of feelings of loss and grief which they cannot express, or are denied, in their communities of origin.

Entering a new community, however, does not automatically grant these women unquestionable membership, and they are exposed to similar practices of inter-evaluation, just as in their communities of origin, in order to ensure internal alignment and consensus. The methods employed to achieve this aim resort to similar affective sanctioning operating in society at large, to minimize heterogeneity and homogenize individuals' experience and practice to the internally held normative standards. Our investigation revealed specific practices of honoring and dishonoring conforming or divergent experiences, underpinning the emergence of key group status markers which signal belonging. We identified three such group status markers. First, there is a reconceptualization of the experience of suffering, which aims to validate the women's loss and grief as legitimate. Second, this process of reconceptualization is permeated by a continuous sanctioning of the correctness or incorrectness of the individuals' accounts of loss and grief shared in the forums. Lastly, we identified the redefinition of personal suffering as happiness at having been able to experience pregnancy at all, regardless of the ultimate outcome. We observed that this becomes a key signifier of group belonging, and presented a description of the processes of realignment, operated by differing individual accounts, to the new hierarchy of feeling norms which is being constituted.

Such a redefinition, we noted, is achieved by a reconceptualization of the status of the 'realness' of the unborn, with the category of Angel baby emerging as a signifier of such an ontological grounding. The commonly accepted use of such a label signals the collective accomplishment of the reality of the unborn. We ended by noting that the constitution of the status of the lost baby as a real baby is pivotal to the collective establishment of a new ethnopsychology of motherhood, which will be signified by the creation of the category of Angel's mother. This emerging category allows for their status as mothers to be accounted for as equally 'real' to that which is granted to those whom they name earth mothers (those women who bear live babies). Ultimately, the emergence of such a reframed ethnopsychology of motherhood generates a new set of feeling norms—by which they must abide—which entitles them to mourn after their loss and validates their sorrow and suffering.

We concluded the empirical investigation by highlighting the feedback loop between the interconnected communities to which these women belong. We identified key elements of the categories of motherhood and babyhood existing in society at large, which anchor the new reframing of the ethnopsychology of motherhood of the bereaved communities. We identified two of these anchoring features as the suffering mother and the reality of the unborn, which have roots in the religious narratives of the Catholic Church adopted in Polish society. We also noted how some elements of the new ethnopsychology of motherhood, emerging from these bereavement communities, travel back to the society at large. With this, we aimed to further illustrate that change is inherent in social life, and that social phenomena should be conceived as in a mode of continuous creation.

Summa summarum, both the analytical framework developed in this book and the empirical study served us to highlight the individualistic bias implicit in most emotion theory and research. We demonstrated that any cultural frame that is placed on individual feelings in fact emerges from the dynamics of interaction, and, thus, should be considered as a collective achievement which circumscribes how interactants construct both emotional subcultures and their own emotional experiences. This process of reconstruction and redefinition of emotional experiences has several key phases. Firstly, individuals collectively identify the lack of subjectively and existentially useful descriptive categories with which they can refer to their feelings in their communities of origin. Secondly, these individuals, collectively as well, attempt to generate new constellations of feelings and categories, which allow for the recognition of their subjective experiences. Thirdly, they achieve this by modifying their own practices and beliefs in relation to the other members of the localized collective. In doing so, they become social agents of a new status group that constitutes a new ethnopsychology; that is, a new emotional life-world which should be perceived as a collective accomplishment, and a collective good, shared by all its members.

Acknowledging the collective and processual dimension of individuals' emotional experiences and behavior enables a particular understanding of agency and action, one that does not focus on individuals themselves (and their set of dispositions imprinted in the process of socialization), but, instead, considers the constitutive role of what is happening between people when 'being with others'. In the perspective we offer, individuals should be perceived as emotionally bound to the group, mutually susceptible to inter-evaluation practices and collective pressures, taking the form of affective sanctioning internal to the groups they wish to belong to. In this process, agency is prior to social structure, in that individuals are constantly calculating, inferring, interpreting, and checking the effects and consequences of their actions with others who surround them. This key conclusion revealed by our analysis has three important practical implications.

First of all, it reveals key features which permeate the dynamics of online bereavement support groups which may be relevant, and valuable, to the moderators of such groups who aim to effectively manage, in a balanced, just, and productive manner, the interactional processes operating in such contexts. In the existing literature on the role of moderators in a variety of online discussions, this role is conceived mainly through their function as filters of the content of computer-mediated communication, or warrantors of the quite vaguely defined quality of internet debates (see e.g. Blumler and Coleman, 2001; Wright and Street, 2007). Based on the analysis presented here, the notion of the quality of supportive communication may be further explored and specified. Moderators of grass-roots online mutual support groups are often recruited from long-term users of the forum, and do not possess any particular professional training (Till, 2003). As a result, they intuitively struggle to channel communication on the forum into what they perceive as model support, and deal with the mechanisms of affective sanctioning and group pressures described earlier.[1] A better understanding of the group processes and interactional mechanisms through which such emotional pressures are exercised could enable the formulation of standards and procedures for moderators, allowing them to derive their activities from a specified—and manageable—model of group processes, rather than personal intuition. In light of the fact that the moderators of online support groups often deal with sensitive and highly emotionally loaded issues (as is the case in online bereavement communities), the development of such procedures or guidelines seems to be an urgent and crucial challenge. We hope that this book, at least partially, will help people in these positions to better deal with such realities, if not by giving clear practical guidelines, by offering insights into the mechanisms underpinning the dynamics of these realities.

Second, the implications of the analysis presented in this book could be used to direct the clinical practice of healthcare professionals, who in their daily routine encounter parents after perinatal loss. Our study documented that medical personnel are still seen as agents of the emotional exclusion of bereaved parents. We argue that medical personnel engaging in practices of emotional exclusion would be, in our view (following Attig's (2004) typology of disenfranchisement practices), an 'empathic',

---

[1] The observations of moderators who participated as interviewees in our study prove that they are intuitively conscious that the group of interactants—although themselves emotionally excluded by their friends, relatives, and the general public—exercises pressure on its members as well. In their own view their task as moderators is to control and ease this pressure.

'political', and 'ethical failure'. By empathic failure, Attig points to the lack of understanding for the bereaved and their suffering, and by political failure he means:

> an abuse of authority as expertise when others presume to know, but do not actually understand, a mourner's suffering or efforts to overcome it. ... an abuse of authority to choose when others presume to decide what is best for a mourner, to limit his or her options in grieving, to control his or her expressions, or to sanction his or her efforts to overcome suffering. (p. 202)

And by ethical failure, he refers to the lack of respect for the bereaved and their feelings. The analysis presented in this book provides an angle to connect certain activities of medical personnel to the feelings they arouse in the bereaved and the reactions they bring about. These reactions can include decisions to join online mutual support groups, to refrain from seeking professional psychological counseling, or to withdraw from offline interactions. Thus, the book renders visible the interactional mechanisms behind the three kinds of failures indicated, and unlocks the possibility of controlling their effects.

Finally, based on the analysis developed in this book, we argue that targeting individuals as isolated entities must necessarily fail. Policy practice should recognize that individual practices and feelings are constituted as collective patterns of behavior. They emerge when individuals orient themselves to others in order to increase their internal group status, perform actions to elicit recognition and deference from others, and avoid those which can bring about a loss of face. It follows, therefore, that emotions in general, and emotions such as pride and shame in particular, must be understood as causal and determining of social life and individual practice, and not only as a product of it. Through the lens of the conceptual framework presented here, grief management ceases to be an individual responsibility, instead becoming a collective endeavor. Contrary to the dominant psychological perspective, in this book we reveal that any successful intervention must aim to monitor and channel group processes, rather than aiming to mold individual feelings and practices. It is the sociological perspective presented here, focused on what is going on *between individuals* when they relate to each other, that allows us to link three dimensions of social life—macro-social phenomena, micro-dynamics of social life, and individual emotional experiences—and understand both their origins and the interplay between them.

BIBLIOGRAPHY

Attig, T. (2004). Disenfranchised Grief Revisited: Discounting Hope and Love. *OMEGA, 49*(3), 197–215.

Blumler, J., & Coleman, S. (2001). *Realising Democracy Online: A Civic Commons in Cyberspace*. Research Publication No 1. London, UK: Institute of Public Policy Research/Citizens Online.

Collins, R. (2005). *Interaction Ritual Chains*. Princeton, NJ: Princeton University Press.

Thomason, B. C. (1982). *Making Sense of Reification. Alfred Schutz and Constructionist Theory*. Hong Kong, HK: The Macmillan Press.

Till, J. E. (2003). *Evaluation of Support Groups for Women with Breast Cancer: Importance of the Navigator Role*. Health Qual Life Outcomes Online Publication 1 May. https://doi.org/10.1186/1477-7525-1-16

Wright, S., & Street, J. (2007). Democracy, Deliberation and Design: The Case of Online Discussion Forums. *New Media Society, 9*(5), 849–869.

BIBLIOGRAPHY

Attig, T. (2004). Disenfranchised Grief Revisited: Discounting Hope and Love. *OMEGA, 49*(3), 197–215.

Austin, J. L. (1970 [1955]). *How to Do Things with Words. The William James Lectures Delivered at Harvard University in 1955.* Oxford, UK: Clarendon Press.

Barnes, B. (1983a). Social Life as Bootstrapped Induction. *Sociology, 17*(4), 524–545.

Barnes, B. (1983b). On the Conventional Character of Knowledge and Cognition. In K. D. Knorr-Cetina & M. Mulkay (Eds.), *Science Observed. Perspectives on the Social Study of Science* (pp. 19–51). London, UK: Sage.

Barnes, B. (1985). Ethnomethodology as Science. *Social Studies of Science, 15*(4), 751–762.

Barnes, B. (1992). Status Groups and Collective Action. *Sociology, 26*(2), 259–270.

Barnes, B. (1995). *The Elements of Social Theory.* London, UK: UCL Press.

Barnes, B. (2001). Practices as Collective Action. In K. D. Knorr-Cetina, T. Schatzki, & E. von Savigny (Eds.), *The Practice Turn in Contemporary Theory* (pp. 17–28). London, UK: Routledge.

Barnes, B., Bloor, D., & Henry, J. (1996). *Scientific Knowledge. A Sociological Analysis.* London, UK: The University of Chicago Press.

Becker, H. S. (1963). *Outsiders: Studies in the Sociology of Deviance.* London, UK: Free Press of Glencoe.

Berger, P. L., & Luckmann, T. (1966). *The Social Construction of Reality: A Treatise in the Sociology of Knowledge.* Harmondsworth, UK: Penguin.

Bernini, S. (2015). Mothers and Children in Post-War Europe: Martyrdom and National Reconstruction in Italy and Poland. *European Review of History: Revue européenne d'histoire, 22*(2), 242–258.

© The Author(s) 2020
I. Rafanell, M. Sawicka, *Emotions in Digital Interactions,*
https://doi.org/10.1007/978-3-030-21998-7

Bloor, D. (1991 [1976]). *Knowledge and Social Imagery*. London, UK and Chicago, IL: The University of Chicago Press.

Bloor, D. (1997a). *Wittgenstein, Rules and Institutions*. London, UK: Routledge.

Bloor, D. (1997b). Collective Representations. In *Images and Reality*. Hungary: Hungarian Academy of Science.

Bloor, D. (1999). Anti-Latour. *Studies in History and Philosophy of Science, 30*(1), 81–112.

Bloor, D. (2001). Wittgenstein and the Priority of Practice. In T. R. Schatzki, K. Knorr-Cetina, & E. von Savigny (Eds.), *The Practice Turn in Contemporary Theory*. London, UK: Routledge.

Blumler, J., & Coleman, S. (2001). *Realising Democracy Online: A Civic Commons in Cyberspace*. Research Publication No 1. London, UK: Institute of Public Policy Research/Citizens Online.

Bourdieu, P. (1990). *In Other Words* (L. J. D. Wacquant, Trans.). Cambridge, UK: Polity Press.

Bourdieu, P. (1994 [1982]). *Distinction. A Social Critique of the Judgement of Taste*. London, UK: Routledge.

Bourdieu, P. (1995 [1980]). *The Logic of Practice*. Cambridge, UK: Polity Press.

Bourdieu, P. (2001 [1998]). *Masculine Domination*. Cambridge, Blackwell.

Braun, V., & Clarke, V. (2006). Using Thematic Analysis in Psychology. *Qualitative Research in Psychology, 3*(2), 77–101.

Burawoy, M. (2018). Making Sense of Bourdieu. *Catalyst, 2*(1), 51–87.

Butler, J. (1990). *Gender Trouble: Feminism and the Subversion of Identity*. London, UK: Routledge.

Butler, J. (1993). *Bodies That Matter: On the Discursive Limits of Sex*. New York, NY: Routledge.

Butler, J. (1994). Gender as Performance. An Interview with Judith Butler. *Radical Philosophy, 67*, 32–39.

CBOS. (2018). *Religijność Polaków i ocena sytuacji Kościoła Katolickiego*. Survey Report No. 147/2018.

Collins, R. (2000). Situational Stratification: A Micro-Macro Theory of Inequality. *Social Theory, 18*(1), 17–43.

Collins, R. (2005). *Interaction Ritual Chains*. Princeton, NJ: Princeton University Press.

Denzin, N. (1990). On Understanding Emotion: The Interpretative-Cultural Agenda. In T. Kemper (Ed.), *Research Agenda for Sociology of Emotions* (pp. 85–116). New York, NY: SUNY.

Durkheim, E. (1982 [1885]). What Is a Social Fact. In S. Lukes (Ed.), *The Rules of Sociological Method and Selected Texts on Sociology and Its Method* (pp. 50–59). London, UK: Macmillan.

Garfinkel, H. (1999 [1967]). *Studies in Ethnomethodology*. Cambridge, UK: Polity Press.

Goffman, E. (1956). Embarrassment and Social Organisation. *American Journal of Sociology, LXII*(3), 264–271.

Gordon, S. (1990). Social Structural Effects on Emotions. In T. Kemper (Ed.), *Research Agenda for Sociology of Emotions* (pp. 145–179). New York, NY: SUNY.

Hazen, M. A. (2003). Societal and Workplace Responses to Perinatal Loss: Disenfranchised Grief or Healing Connection. *Human Relations, 56*(2), 147–166.

Heidegger, M. (2011 [1927]). *Being and Time* (J. Macquarrie & E. Robinson, Trans.). New York, NY: Harper & Row.

Heritage, J. (2008 [1984]). *Garfinkel and Ethnomethodology.* Cambridge, UK: Polity Press.

Hochschild, A. R. (2003). *The Managed Heart. Commercialization of Human Feeling.* Berkeley, CA: University of California Press.

Jackson, S., & Jones, J. (1998). *Contemporary Feminist Theories.* Edinburgh, UK: Edinburgh University Press.

James, W. R. (2000). Placing the Unborn: On the Social Recognition of New Life. *Anthropology & Medicine, 7*(2), 169–189.

Keefe-Cooperman, K. (2004 [2005]). A Comparison of Grief as Related to Miscarriage and Termination for Fetal Abnormality. *OMEGA, 50*(4), 281–300.

Kusch, M. (2002). *Knowledge by Agreement.* Oxford, UK: Oxford University Press.

Lang, A., Fleiszer, A. R., Duhamel, F., Sword, W., Gilbert, K. R., & Corsini-Munt, S. (2011). Perinatal Loss and Parental Grief: The Challenge of Ambiguity and Disenfranchised Grief. *OMEGA, 63*(2), 183–196.

Livingston, E. (1987). *Making Sense of Ethnomethodology.* London, Routledge.

Lofland, L. H. (1985). The Social Shaping of Emotion: The Case of Grief. *Symbolic Interaction, 8*(2), 171–190.

Maynard, D., & Clayman, S. E. (1991). The Diversity of Ethnomethodology. *Annual Review of Sociology, 17*, 385–418.

Rafanell, I. (2009). Durkheim and the Performative Model: Reconfiguring Social Objectivity. In G. Cooper, A. King, & R. Rettie (Eds.), *Sociological Objects: The Reconfiguration of Social Theory* (pp. 59–76). Farnham, UK: Ashgate.

Rafanell, I. (2013). Micro-Situational Foundations of Social Structure: An Interactionist Exploration of Affective Sanctioning. *Journal for the Theory of Social Behaviour, 43*(2), 181–204.

Rafanell, I. (2021). *Making up Bodies: Sexed and Gendered Bodies as Social Institutions.* London, UK: Palgrave Macmillan.

Rafanell, I., & Gorringe, H. (2010). Consenting to Domination? Theorising Power, Agency and Embodiment with Reference to Caste. *The Sociological Review, 58*(4), 604–622.

Rawls, A. (2003). Harold Garfinkel. In G. Ritzer (Ed.), *The Blackwell Companion to Major Contemporary Social Theorists* (pp. 89–124). Maden, TN: Blackwell Publishing.

Sauder, M. (2005). Symbols and Contexts: An Interactionist Approach to the Study of Social Status. *The Sociological Quarterly, 46*(1), 279–298.

Sawicka, M. (2017). Searching for a Narrative of Loss: Interactional Ordering of Ambiguous Grief. *Symbolic Interaction, 40*(2), 229–246.

Scheff, T. J. (1988). Shame and Conformity: The Deference-Emotion System. *American Sociological Review, 53*(June), 395–406.

Scheff, T. J. (2000). Shame and the Social Bond: A Sociological Theory. *Sociological Theory, 18*(1), 84–99.

Schutz, A. (1962). *The Phenomenology of the Social World.* Evanston, IL: Northwestern University Press.

Thoits, P. A. (1989). The Sociology of Emotions. *Annual Review of Sociology, 15*, 317–342.

Thoits, P. A. (1990). Emotional Deviance. In T. Kemper (Ed.), *Research Agenda for Sociology of Emotions* (pp. 180–203). New York, NY: SUNY.

Thomas, W. I. (1928). *The Child in America: Behavior Problems and Programs.* New York, NY: Knopf.

Thomason, B. C. (1982). *Making Sense of Reification. Alfred Schutz and Constructionist Theory.* Hong Kong, HK: The Macmillan Press.

Till, J. E. (2003). *Evaluation of Support Groups for Women with Breast Cancer: Importance of the Navigator Role.* Health Qual Life Outcomes Online Publication 1 May. https://doi.org/10.1186/1477-7525-1-16

Trochimczyk, M. (2003). Mater Dolorosa and Maternal Love in Górecki's Music. *Polish Music Journal* (6)2, Online Publication. Retrieved March 20, 2019, from https://polishmusic.usc.edu/research/publications/polish-music-journal/vol6no2/mater-dolorosa-and-maternal-love-in-goreckis-music/

Wierzbicka, A. (1999). *Emotions Across Languages and Cultures: Diversity and Universals.* Cambridge, UK: Cambridge University Press.

Wikan, U. (1990). *Managing Turbulent Hearts: A Balinese Formula for Living.* Chicago, IL: The University of Chicago Press.

Wittgenstein, L. (1953). *Philosophical Investigations.* Oxford, UK: Blackwell Publishing.

Wright, S., & Street, J. (2007). Democracy, Deliberation and Design: The Case of Online Discussion Forums. *New Media Society, 9*(5), 849–869.

INDEX[1]

[1] Note: Page numbers followed by 'n' refer to notes.

© The Author(s) 2020
I. Rafanell, M. Sawicka, *Emotions in Digital Interactions*,
https://doi.org/10.1007/978-3-030-21998-7

117